DELINQUENT

FUTUREPOEM BOOKS
NEW YORK CITY
2009

DELINQUENT
Mina Pam Dick

Copyright © 2009 Pam Dick
ISBN: 978-0-9822798-1-6

FIRST EDITION | FIRST PRINTING

This edition first published in paperback by Futurepoem books
P.O. Box 7687 JAF Station, NY, NY 10116
www.futurepoem.com
Series Editor: Dan Machlin
Guest Editors: Tan Lin, Frances Richard, Jerome Sala

Cover design: Mickel Design (http://www.mickeldesign.com)
Cover image: Nico Pam Dick

Typesetting & copyediting: *type*slowly design (cjmattison@gmail.com)
Typefaces: National, by Kris Sowersby (Spine & Back Cover); Eldorado & Dante (Text)
Printed in the United States of America on acid-free paper

NYSCA
New York State Council on the Arts

This project is supported by grants from the New York State Council on the Arts, a state agency, the New York Community Trust, and The Fund for Poetry, as well as individual donors and subscribers. Futurepoem books is the publishing program of Futurepoem, Inc., a New York State-based 501(c)3 non-profit organization dedicated to creating a greater public awareness and appreciation of innovative literature.

Distributed to the trade by Small Press Distribution, Berkeley, California
Toll-free number (U.S. only): 800.869.7553
Bay area/International: 510.524.1668
orders@spdbooks.org
www.spdbooks.org

Acknowledgments:

Many thanks to Futurepoem editors Dan Machlin, Frances Richard, Tan Lin and Jerome Sala—in particular, to Dan, Frances and Tan for their insightful notes. Thanks to Jeremy Mickel for cover design and Peter Hall and Cris Mattison for copy-editing/typesetting. Thanks to Yasmine Alwan, generous and supportive editor of *Tantalum*, for publishing prior versions of 'St. Frances by Sassetta' and selections from 'Some Instants.' Likewise to Donald Breckenridge at *The Brooklyn Rail* for publishing 'The Crumbs.' Thanks to Larry Fagin for early enthusiasm and criticism. Thanks to Matvei Yankelevich for ardent bar talks and exposure to great weird authors. Thanks to Robert, Franz, Søren, Ludwig, the Friedrichs, Georg, Rainer, Fyodor and Benedict for inspiration. Thanks to Sylvia and Bob for steadfastness and hilarity. Thanks to Michael, my father, my mother and Bill for their belief and encouragement. Thanks to my father for his influence. Above all, thanks to Thessia for her everything and then some.

For Thessia

It is with the subjective thinker as it is with a writer and his style; for he only has a style who never has anything finished . . .

—Johannes Climacus/Søren Kierkegaard

Contents

I. Variations

3	The Imaginary Unit Persists
4	The Infinite Benjamina
7	St. Francis by Sassetta
8	Some Instants
12	Clara sequence (Cs)—a Lyrical Element
31	Shame Is Shameless
32	A Figment
40	Lens
41	Bad Posture
42	Hildegard the Unsteady
49	Daughter & Father
49	Sleeping Beauty
49	Unrated
50	The Crumbs

II. Deviations

57	The Agnes Splinters
61	The Scrapped Book of Minna Maude Ingvar
66	First Person of Truth
81	Philosophical Scrap
100	The Felix

I. VARIATIONS

The Imaginary Unit Persists

Once I was a knight, they called me Sir Hermina, informally Mina. I sported a lance and wore a midriff. Recall that iced coffee is cold. Hair should be washed every other day. No! In my SRO, I live amongst big fakers. The tunesmiths filled the hallways. Unrepentant ambling. What is wrong with a harem? A red dress, a white one and a brown one. Actually, tunics, and my ladies were gentlemen. Like Kierkegaard, Kafka and Walser, I am a steadfast bachelor. Like Kierkegaard, Nietzsche and Schopenhauer, I am a stubborn unemployee. My problem is emotion—they say I squander equanimity. Yet much is left, although all is already written. Personally, I exist to dot their i's and cross their t's. T for truth, i for the square root of -1, which is imaginary. I need to trim my fingernails and toenails. Neither mental nor personal hygiene. Nu, and dental? Forget that. It's time to be dreamy. There are no mountains here. Perhaps in France or Switzerland. Also the Waldau Sanatorium outside Berne. I will take with me my pale green Hermes Rocket typewriter made in Switzerland in the year of my birth. They have rec rooms. I debuted as Don Giovanni or Faust or a split-second Antigone. The adventures splintered. A shaved head raises courage. Prod the issue with twigs. A tree here or there, a wall, an illegal firearm. I, Mina, persisted in willful romantic musings. Many are chosen, few are called. An aristocrat of yore gets impoverished, but destitution suits me. The men appreciated my nonchalant affections, the ladies liked my curlicues. Mountain peaks twitched, clouds parted, a rod of sunlight pushed me. On the stage, a lackeyish bow. To stuttered claps, I exited. Reencounter myself here, listening to the raving bum by the moat. Dash it!

The Infinite Benjamina

Benjamina the Hermit

Guilt is good. Since they're angry, you can snowball. I messed up my contact lens. They might arrest me for improper documents. A cell is a cell; saints have done worse. I might cave in when I shut up. Contrast Plato to the two St. Anthonys. Once, I had an intention. My mind makes *me* up. This asinine wit will not be canonized, nor this busy loneliness beatified.

Benjamina the Elder

Benjamina amongst the teenagers: warmth makes her fester. Why be privy to that? Donuts and cameras play innocent. The snow-glazed twigs were more Benjamina's thing. But don't haul weather to mortals. I outlived my welcome. Is there another possible speech balloon? Blink in fear.

Benjamina the Free-Willed

When Benjamina came downstairs, the world tried to flummox her. She lived onward. Polish people are Catholics in lemon-colored clothing. What solace. I love New York again, still I must go. Bum rush or be a good customer. World rose up again insouciantly. I possess all the necessities, even though my tooth aches. Life's warp and woof are things over which we can existentially quantify in logic, if they're variables. One eyebrow down. Two elbows out. Car horn. Church bell. Passersby of the odious variety. My hair stinks from watchman's thinking cap. Lookers vs. thinkers. Let it be this vs. let this be it.

Benjamina the Morbid

Springtime is the right time to lay hands on yourself. The buds rejoicing. Benjamina Ens—her last name rhymes with spring in unrenowned German, thereby with the figurative prime of life, which is dubious. Who said I believed in free or unfree verse? Clever ones tremble. It would be something to be smooth and simple like an olive. Black outline on a white ground. Words show no pity.

Benjamina the Reader

Jakob Michael Reinhold Lenz howled up and down the mountain. O joy and angst! His lenses were bifocals. *Vide* Benedict de Spinoza's grindwork, but beware of tiny glass splinters. A rue *sub specie aeternitatis* could be the same mode as a coughing fit. Synthetic identity statements are crucial, as recognized Gottlob and Benjamina. The morning star = the evening star. My end = my beginning. Last = first. Georg was bipolar. Poor Jakob Michael could not revive the little dead girl. He was no supplanter. Ach, who is like God? Verses wept.

Benjamina the Witness

Khaki-toned boy on yellow bike pops a wheelie at the bus shelter. I should be impressed? Maybe. Squatters wave electric bass banners. The 13-year-old carrot-top from my building, suddenly adeptly leather-jacketed—I christened him Ginger. He stayed shy. It's a day of parades, alluring fleshy Jessicas and devil-may-care fallen arches. A strong back. Closet daintiness. Bodies with rubber footwear to guard against shocks. Los Hermanos de St. Martini de Porres in purple robes marched in a slow-mo diagonal argument. The reals are uncountable. Synchronized sinning. A saint with a chip on his shoulder blessed 12th street. Little girls in white angel costumes tripped over themselves to be first to reach sweetness. Benjamina nodded politely to the head-scarved old Latinas who were not surprised to see her, since they didn't. The B-52s are also superb, and celebration is the Logos. I sided with Heraclitus for two minutes that were homologous with eternity. Long live clattering dishes! Those with ears to hear should listen. Why isn't joy weird? Then I grew bored. You had to be there. Shrank to a cuticle on the left hand of God. Better that than to a son of man under the right hand. Benjamina no more! On to the escape clause. It's prepositional and probably dependent.

St. Francis by Sassetta

T-shirts feel reluctance. Bad people spend money. I removed one and thrust it at a beggar. This action did not lead to the blond androgynous architectural sleep, nor to the humble *a posteriori* fontanelle of a transfigured bald spot. If you can remove your eyeballs, do so. If not, try poking them with a finger. Things grew blurry as I kept up with appearances but did not save them. One thumbed a yellowed copy and wandered. Certain pronouns become obsolete. Is that poverty?

Innocent Moment

The girl blinked rapidly, stared down to the left and pulled on a strand of her stringy fair hair. She wore a light blue t-shirt with the words *John Denver* and a photo of the towheaded country singer John Denver on it, and nearby a metal fan rattled and somebody coughed. John Denver dyed his hair. For a second, I quit existing.

The Talent

A young man sat curling and uncurling his left hand while doing nothing with his right hand. Then he switched to curling and uncurling his right hand while not troubling with his left. His name was probably Daniil.

Exultation

I ran across the street at the flashing light to catch up to the kids in safety-orange doublets. They came from the Children's Liberation day care center, their teachers were full-hipped, generously haunched, and spoke Spanish or English, and I, too, wished to be a liberated child! But I was already a teenager. The 4-year-olds held hands with one another, I held hands with God, i.e., Jesus Christ, i.e., the pubescent boy whom St. Catherine of Alexandria married in a pure mystical union. She was a philosopher. Furthermore, for once my toasted onion bagel was buttered correctly. Yeah, rejoice! Leaves sang the chorus.

Fellows

Caspar David Friedrich said, *I love my fellow man, but to love him I must stay far away from him.* He painted mountains with the backs of figures staring at them or standing on them. Young Kaspar Hauser stood alone in his closet, dreaming a perfect outside world. The backs of heads are highly spiritual and full of mystery, it's good to stroke them. In their closet of an apartment, Gaspar and his father read each other the Bible's fairy tales, such that Gaspar was neither lonely nor lacking in language. Then I was Gaspar, not Minna. Please stay over on that bench. The dogs howled angrily, although they were supposed to be playing. Soon it shall rain. Sharing the weather is a supreme intimacy.

Modest Malaise

Greta under a dark morning sky, attacked by a feeling of dread, a wriggling visual field and a fierce impulse to run away quickly. Will I collapse in a fit? If only it were epilepsy, as Julius Caesar, Prince Myshkin and Fyodor Dostoevsky had! But it's mere hypoglycemic faintness. Therefore no flash of light or spiritual epiphany precedes the attacks; rather, the sensation of agitated nerves is prominent. From this a frantic darkness results, until some item such as a cracker or pretzel or chocolate bar is acquired.

Renown

Once a king had an illegitimate daughter named Eamona. Nickname Mona. Now, one day, she . . . Oh never mind. What interest could a bastard girl's actions hold for the reading public? The prince and royal heir had a cleft chin, a harelip and a learning disability, isn't that what's fascinating? Exit bastard. Her boots clomped like fists upon a table. The Last Supper excluded girls—where were the various Marys? I should get a job at the nearby Woolworth's selling bras, panties, washcloths, towels. They won't like my short haircut. I'll secure a Greek boyfriend and tear away with him on his motorcycle, my arms around his boxy rib cage. He will read Herman Hesse to me, and my life shall be different ever after. I made several mistakes, not all of them were visible. When the sunlight returns, use a toothpick, then go for an afternoon *Wanderjahre*. Do not forget to proclaim where you live, or why. In six worlds or less. They keep disowning them. The former planet hung abashed in the galaxy.

The Mystery of No Mystery

A girl grew up a believer, one minute in puberty she turned into an unbeliever. Some said it was too much children's cereal such as Trix, some said raging hormones, some blamed her new haircut: a bob with idiot bangs. Getting to third base with Seymour in the Planetarium served as consolation and theoretical datum. Yet the mental causes the mental and the physical causes the physical, according to Spinoza. Furthermore, underneath, it's all logical entailment. The girl's zipper got caught from the beginning of time, the mode of her zipper's getting caught was necessary. Thus good. But since this girl had no conviction, the shame of the situation was a given. Besides, Spinoza's God is really an unbeliever's God, why else was he excommunicated? At least he felt calm and happy. O that existence could unfurl as a plush royal carpet upon which we'd stroll, slowly and grandly, luxuriating in the comfort of ceremony. The floor of the Planetarium was carpeted, therefore not too cold on the accidentally bared skin of the lower back. Instead of tranquility, a great excitement ruled the land. Every year, God flunks out of junior high. Whereas philosophy is like coming attractions.

Clara sequence (Cs)—a Lyrical Element

1
The day rolls Clara into a thin prone sheet.
It doesn't roll her so thin that she tears.

2
Before, Clara was lustrous.
Not all metals stay the same.

3
old-fashioned female easy chair with dainty feet and a yellow floral curved body

4
on its side in the gutter until male orderlies cart it away in the white ambulance

5
no sanitation truck

6
It's not the case that Clara lies in the gutter.
Clara has a name, it is Clara.

7
Not all truths are logical—true by form.
Both ambulance cars and sanitation trucks are white.

8
White does not blot out yellow.
Typically, Clara is white.

9
clear-toned chirp of dull-toned bird

10
dark blue t-shirt with white number 17 on the back

11
There's a helicopter landing on Clara.
There's no helicopter landing on Clara.

12
double mattress in the gutter

13
off-white with deep impressions

14
fleeting or lasting indents, cf. Clara

15
slight of frame, older than 17

16
Wittgenstein's slight frame, Frege's slight frame, Clara's slight frame

17
Frege's slight frame?

18
his hirsute jaw vs. Wittgenstein's clean-shaven jaw vs. Clara's smooth jaw

19
sense vs. force vs. tone

20
pure tone vs. alloy

21
Wittgenstein was not sure his tone was male by form.
Of two bird tones, one is higher than the other.

22
bird meaning female in English English being a stale thought for Clara like garbage

23
killing two birds with one Wittgenstein

24
Typically, birds are killed by boys or men.

It isn't often that boys or men get killed by birds.

25
A robin's nest was in a tree.

The tree was not really a tree.

26
A weed only has meaning in the context of a sentence such as a garden.

It's not true that life and death aren't sentences.

27
three turquoise blue eggs in a nest

28
three pearl grey men around a tree

29

Then the tree was cut down, so it became a weed.

The eggs with the nest did not survive.

30

Clara fell into despair and died for a day.

The falling of a tree is not identical to the falling of a Clara.

31

Despair obscures luster.

Obscurity is not always illustrious.

32

Gottlob, Ludwig, Clara = brilliance, glory, brightness.

Brightness ≠ brilliance, glory.

33

Milky Way candy bar in dark wrapper with glowing stars and the words *Midnight Dark*

34

Clara's age is two times the number on Clara's back.

Clara was not sure her tone was grown up by logic.

35
'Do not litter,' 'Don't you litter?' and 'I want you not to litter' share a component sense—you don't litter—which is made clear in the following: 'Make it the case that you don't litter,' 'Is it the case that you don't litter?' and 'I want it to be the case that you don't litter'—littering being bad.

A component is not the whole.

36
Then how could it express it?

37
the same for an element

38
A question is not a positive or negative assertion.

Clara has curly light brown hair like a cloud of electrons.

39
a phrase not an assertion

40
empirical truth of Clara's being over 17

41
logical truth of canary yellow's being yellow

42
I am Clara.
I am not covered with canary yellow feathers.

43
I do not lay eggs.
I do say bad thoughts.

44
If laying an egg means saying a bad thought, then I do lay eggs.
Philosophers are not wholes.

45
Clara had meaning only in the context of a sentence.
She was not independent of the world.

46
But the inverse?

47
The world is neutral.
'The world is neutral' is not a convincing assertion.

48
milky cloudiness of Milky Way starlight in the Milky Way galaxy, *galaxy* meaning milk

49
Clara pulling on her square upper lip, Clara not scratching her balls (cf. 'The king of France is bald')

50
Truth equals positive, falsity equals negative.
That's not the set-up.

51
chemical not logical necessity

52
The bird laying the turquoise-toned eggs was not necessarily a robin.
Ludwig and Gottlob became famous.

53
Gottblob: a typo

54
Robin, i.e., diminutive male or female bright frame—no, fame—

55
There exist typos.
Discussion of the sense of the name *Robin* isn't new, aka young.

56
Garbage turns rotten.
It is not right to litter the world with a mass of garbage.

57
The mass is a number like the atomic number but different.
Inertia of the mass need not be negative.

58
The mess is a number?

59
My sequence is nearly half-over already.
It is never too late to turn significant.

60
weight vs. wait

61
a soft and ductile pupil

62
Robin Hood was a star—a famous outlaw who lived where he shouldn't, in the context of trees.
There was no famous law or outcast or star pupil named Clara.

63
silvery metal

64
malleable alloys of sidewalks

65
in summer or winter, suffering of vagrants

66
Cf. means compare.
A hammer which hammered on Clara did not break her.

67
the starving tattered man with torn teeth impressing Clara deeply

68
lack of transparency of the metal a person or thing is made of, or of their context

69

electric current and heat or hot and electric thoughts and feelings flowing through Clara

70

aggregate of glints

71

The Electric Company (on television) & Clara, age 5 (in front of television)

72

Ludwig & Gottlob qua light bulbs

73

I want to be a girl again.

Clara did not follow the pretty blond shirtless skateboarder.

74

Claribel is an old-fashioned name, *Clarinda* is unusual.

Clara didn't wear an old-fashioned white dickey.

75

inserted dickeybird of one old thought

76
'I want to be a youth again,' said the thought.
The thought did not have any more teeth.

77
You need to keep track of where you are or you will make a mistake.
It's not good to be lost.

78
tract being a pamphlet, therefore on love

79
Tractatus of Ludwig, tractability of Clara

80
She was forgetful because impressionable.
That boy's name was not Sebastian.

81
yellowed mattress plus the thought, 'I will not know how to stop this'

82
A bird laid three blue eggs in the nest of Clara's light brown curly hair.
It's no accident that *chick*, like *bird*, means girl.

83
The chicks' names were *sense*, *force* and *tone*.
I do not know how to theorize language.

84
Or else one bird died, the other two were dubbed *sense* and *reference*.
Clara does not know how to theorize language.

85
sweat of people who shine when hot

86
The sheen on Clara had grown clouded.
Charlie Sheen (boy) does not equal Martin Sheen (man).

87
that boy's name not being Charlie, Charlie being now a man with a shiny bald globe

88
the Planetarium

89
class trips necessitating docility

90
The world is my own planet which I am on.
The world is not only all that is the case.

91
Ludwig shrugged off Gottlob, Clara shrugged off Ludwig.
Ludwig did not stay a school teacher.

92
slapping a little girl's hand with his standard ruler or ignoring her

93
I do not wish to be a girl again.
I am now a grown-up.

94
old Italian man with crooked stairwell nose and eyes on different stories

95
old Chinese man collecting plastic bottles and singing tones in his scale with its tightly massed notes

96
illogical connectives of the park, a leafy garden

97
treatise of experience of innocence

98
Stevie the boy was 14.
Clara is not 14 anymore.

99
yellow teeth or belly

100
off-white instead of yellow Clara

101
You should be brave every day.
It is not too late to be brave.

102
Then she went downstairs.
It wasn't possible to keep going while starved of phenomena.

103
But what if this is a terrible mistake and ruins everything so it turns into garbage?

104

Clara could be cast off- -as with her treatise—like scrap metal.

It's not too late to be new.

105

Clara went down to the world.

The world did not destroy Clara.

106

Birds are thoughts in the mind which is an aviary, according to Plato.

Plato did not feel ashamed of falling in Platonic love with beautiful boys.

107

her head flying off with inspiration

108

little kids counting down with shouts thrown by the breeze

109

lanky brunet man in a white butcher's novice smock, smoking in front of the butcher's shop

110

children and adults entering butcher shops

111
Socrates believed that children knew things they didn't know they knew.
Socrates did not believe that he knew anything.

112
I forget what I knew once.
The world does not remind me.

113
legs as parentheses, arms as brackets: (), {}

114
parking cop like the numeral *1* as seen by a lowercase *x*

115
Latin song by a building that slouched red with its chest protector

116
set of all of Clara's percepts on the avenue between two streets, obfuscated

117
The world does not know itself.
Clara tried to see something.

118
Then logic was rigid like a ruler or a hard-on.
Not always is thinking supple.

119
metal braces on crooked pubescent teeth

120
classes such as math, chemistry, astronomy—concerning the Milky Way

121
If the name for the component also signifies the whole, cannot the component?

122
idea of which ideas might orbit

123
The counterman did not spill when adding milk to the other girl's iced coffee.
Milk existed.

124
Milk flew out of the head of the diminutive genius in the playground.
Trees did not argue.

125
scraping skateboard with the wiry youth with long medium brown hair

126
Clara vs. the two St. Claras, the two crutches of St. Claras, one for each ascetic and ecstatic armpit, now trash in the gutter

127
this *Tractatus* neither logical nor theological

128
the world as alloy (what the fall is)

129
Could a truth tree rise in a Clara if no one else perceived it?

130
rasping of skateboards while thoughts spurt from her eyes, turning into things

131
I do not want to end yet!
I love the world.

132
Clara!

133
The br—

Shame Is Shameless

For a dollar I'll suck your Bic, says Pete, if it's black, dark blue or green. I'm not into the red ones. On the other hand, progress remains alluring. I happened by a whirlwind, it could be Pentecostal or only calamitous. Either way, nice roar. Beige cassocks support feet in tawdry black suede cowboy boots. I sang a whole opera in two minutes, made the most of my androgyny and mood swings. I can't stop grinning, I don't know why. Somebody took their all-natural laundry soap for a walk. It's good to be alive, even leashed. I, too, yearn for a baby blue or mint green or Yoo-hoo brown Vespa. But I'm not sufficiently mechanical, I can't even perform a decision procedure to see if less is more. Meanwhile, meanwhile! Can I finally momentarily contain everything? If so, why? If not, why not? Hey, why shouldn't I? Then, distracted, I try to cover my butt crack which has its crowning hair patch, given that I am a hirsute young man. Aagh, not that again. Don't make an ass of yourself, Pete! I just did. Oh brother! I said slut, didn't I? And proud of it. Watch me fondle adverbs. Tenderly. In Paradise, even shame is shameless. We dig the fig leaf.

A Figment

If...

If.
If only.
If then.
Only if.
Iff (if and only if).
If you say so.
Iffy.

Party

I stood at a party, I was surrounded by revelers. They huddled with their elbows thrust into my ribs, back and chest, oblivious. The sides of their heads did not make me want to caress them. Panic. I began to whirl. A lost and desperate dervish. They enjoyed the newly wrought breeze. Didn't ask questions. I spun, rose above them—so slowly they wouldn't notice. Dove into an orbit around the building. Luckily we were on the roof, or I would have hit the walls and ceiling. Here, I could move in a loyal yet secretly rebellious ellipse. I was preparing. When their eyes fixed on a tumbling comet with a flashy tail, I made my escape.

Lens

The breaths of the stupid ones who blabbed only of themselves fogged Liza. Then God could no longer see through her, so He went to find a better pair of spectacles.

Beforehand

The coming event—an afternoon *tête-à-tête*—hung over my head like the flashing blade of a guillotine. How I wished to rush to it and give it my bare neck, the sooner to return to the daily afterlife of my dream.

Agony of Expectation

The coming event—a dusk parley—loomed before me like some horrible aunt's great perfumed bosom. How I longed to bury my head in it and get it over with. A plan is a form of private torture, only your thoughts wound your feelings.

Isolato

It became clear to Cora that she did not belong there. So, as soon as the last match was struck and the marijuana cigarette lit, she turned into the empty matchbook. Shiny light blue cover, matte white inside, square, closed again, lying peacefully on the cluttered table. Perfectly useless now. And nameless. Stamped with the label *Henryk's Bar* as a diversionary tactic. Slowly recovering from the greasy fumblings of index finger and thumb.

Iteration

Enough already! Enough already!

Relaxation

I take a deep breath. Because I have typed some, I am able to take a deep breath now. *Bertha* is an anagram for *breath*. But that isn't due to me, Bertha. But sometimes I forget that. I think, God is telling me something. After all, I am what went into the first human figurines' nose holes, to bring them to life. Without me, the world would be dumb and brute.

Comparison of Modals

Could is flirtatious, *would* is haunting, but *should* is a knockout.

At the Prom

Should is the blonde bombshell, *could* is the homecoming queen, but *would* is the slumped wallflower whose charms are eternal. Unlike a real flower's.

Don't Fool Yourself

At the end, there shall be no sudden recognition and prize. The ones you do not love will not cry at your graveside. Shouldn't you rejoice over that? Coincidentally, the church bells from St. Stanislaus rang out. But Herman hung his head and bit his lower lip. It's hard to live as a Herman.

Herman Osbert

What happened to the youth named Herman Osbert? He was invented, then he disappeared. He got swept away on the tide of impressions. *Herman* means army man: a horde lived inside Herman Osbert. *Osbert* means god bright, but also raven, a crow variant, if you believe in abbreviations. Herman was like Lisa Bright and Dark, the crazy teenage girl from that book who hid under a school desk muttering or jumped on top of it and ripped her t-shirt off and wiggled her small titties. A crow flies out of the cloud of unknowing, which is the cloud of despair and agony. It (the crow) feels hungry.

Too Late

The park starts to come too much to life. The fleshy people crush the ideas of people under their feet.

Park at the End of the Day: a Meditation

It's different from the park in the morning. Young bum insults you. Old man with tiny bag of potato chips chews as if crashing cymbals. Baton of a dried leafy branch rolls out from under the bench, exorting you to join the marching band yet informing you that it's too late: everyone's dead. Dusk sun makes you and the bench cast one splotchy shadow . . . But all that's a thin memory. Now in my garret. Church bell clanging. Typewriter clacking. The park in the infancy of evening like the white paper stick of a lollipop licked and sucked to its finale. Wet, grimy, useless. Toss it away, go in search of new sweets.

Observation

Exultant shouters flash their shiny syllables and wag their weight around. Resentful mutes hide their subvocalizing and burnish their thinness.

Disgust with Oneself: a Confession

Sometimes the fanciful is like an overly sweet homemade birthday cake produced by a stepbrother whose feelings one is afraid to hurt. So you accept it with a crooked grin. Wish we were an orphan eating a dessert stolen from a bakery. I should become a runaway!

Park at the End of the Day, or Disgust with Another: an Argument

It's different from etc. Slob of a mustachioed man leers and grabs his crotch. We think: He isn't seeing me but only his private mental representation of me. He's making a lewd gesture toward some part of himself—a pure visual content. Then we think: But he himself is just my mental content—some part of me is making a lewd gesture at myself! Next we think, Ach, philosophy! Meanwhile the man pats his bulge with proud hostility. We quit thinking. Bear our visual field away to safety. Conclusion: Don't think; book!

Plea

I would like to be Herman now, if you don't mind. It will only take a minute. Oh, of course; be my guest. In fact, Herman was waiting just for you. He's crouched under the desk.

But Who—?

But who is Herman Osbert? Feckless question. Could be an old guy sitting in the park of an afternoon, eating a bialy. Could be a kid tugging on his shoelaces. Could be an infant flaunting a golden birthmark. First I wrote *bookmark*.

Things in the Life of Herman

A thick orange coaster that clatters when it tumbles.
A green t-shirt.
Two dirty socks.
A subjectivist theory of truth.
A long tongue.
Disheveled dark hair.
A pale green Swiss typewriter.
A thin and elegant Swiss watch of yore.
A daydream about Switzerland, where Robert Walser lived once.
An ink stain.
A coffee stain.
A prattling baby.
A gurgling refrigerator.
A thought of Carl.
A fantasy about Coraline.
Sunlight on the grimy white window sill.
A hopeless knowledge that nothing will ever be finished, ever.
The tweets of birds.
A phobia of plots.

A Few Similes

Herman haunted these pages like the ghost of Christmas Past.
The fog rolled through the avenue like an ice cream truck.
The white t-shirt flapped like an old lady's neck.
The spine of the girl curved like a parenthesis.
The thought fled from me like a disaster victim.
The shout monopolized me like a memory.
The day bristled like somebody you've offended.
Your head vibrated like a guitar string plucked by an aggravated kid in his Thursday afternoon lesson.

Klepto

Somebody filched two pages from me! My left ankle. Now I have to hobble.

Quirk

The elbow was the most poignant part of the body to Herman. It would not be a mistake but instead a sin to analyze why.

Otherwise Engaged

The tall olive-skinned guy with thick wavy dark hair, Roman nose, long limbs, sexy jeans and black sneakers will never like me, thought Minna. I have no tits, I wear glasses, I am a slattern. I am brown-haired, surely he wants a redhead. I am intense, surely he wants somebody fun. So Minna let him lope away, she didn't nudge him. The truth is, his arrogant anti-heroism would have revolted her after a paucity of days. Anyway, she was busy being Herman, who had his eye set on Coraline or perhaps Carl.

Close Call

I almost knocked over my iced coffee with a careless wave of my right forearm. That would have been a terrible sign, a sign of being cursed, even doomed. But preventing it is not a sign of grace. Wherefore this asymmetry of portents?

I, Minna

Some call me selfish, I call myself inspired. Hermaneutics furnishes my good works.

Think About It This Way

If I were a thumb I would want to be sucked. What do I care about some girl's future buck teeth?

Warning

When my first tooth falls out, that will be the sign that I should finally abandon myself. After all, I am no child, I am a grown-up.

The Truth

Did I already say that I am a figment? Furthermore, Herman Osbert is not the only one who exists.

For Instance

For instance, there is Bartholomew.

RW Or Cut?

Rw or cut?

Coda

RW means right worshipful and right worthy as well as rewrite, according to my dictionary. It means Robert Walser according to my dickshunary. The philosophy of abbreviations yields many truths.

P.S. (i.e., Postscript)

Now on to Herbert or Myrna or Dunstan. The lone afterlife is a new name.

Lens

The twentieth Eliza traversed the peaks. They were blocks. None wailing. Snow except for grey concrete. Brown tree branches, dropped bus passes. This music is stupid. The sun stuck a finger out and poked the forest in the eye. It hurt somewhat. I need to buy a new pen, this one has a disorder. Ganglia of trees. Nervous ticking of wooden floorboards. Snow lay all across the berm by the run-over futon. Eliza Lens in her Hessian boots crunched across the room. Don't pull the blinds up, someone might accuse you of a murder. Sun could take revenge. Elsewhere the clouds made a face at Eliza, it was holy. Then a leering grin. Representational art, i.e., religion is infantile. Also Eliza. Annunciations need speech ribbons. Walls decide what to do. We went further. Clouds predicted answers. Wild restlessness with different implements. Or the dull hollow stroke. A wish to write inside out. It snowed upward. One day had a crevice, the other not. Eliza noted the humidity. Nearby, a toy barked. The rattling of the radiator's teeth expresses the anxiety of the room. Get back to the mountains. There the way was up or down. Now I thought indifferently. Pubic hair atop trees. Unlike the others, I am so tired. Lie down, Eliza. She reclined under a blanket of heavy snow. It had snapped the bough off. But Eliza walked across the sheet of paper. It was snow-white. My lazy eye wandered. Eliza wet and cold. Deathly quiet across the land. The slope bears a coefficient. Eliza is inefficient because she forgets herself. Should have snuck into that math class. I will never learn anything. Once a student but quit. Mused somebody with a tightening chest. Grammatical moods darkened.

Bad Posture

Tall, t-shirted and sweet or short, besleeved and manly. On high, a bald advocate. Spill milk on the floor and cry like a baby on the inside. Wall-to-wall ochre carpeting connotes bulging pubescent kisses and slobbering grown-up divorces. Some hunches are built to last. He drank water like a convict, smiled sheepishly at the singer formerly known as Dorothy. *It might be time to go to jail soon*, I said to the lady in black. Dead Johnny crooned from the courtyard. One woman wore a lacy white doily for a shirt. She was nice anyway, so I cleaved to her. I try to forget. I pledge, I will be a tabula rasa. But the Ramones drawing still lurks underneath, & I still wanna be sedated! Get me out before I confess. The world bobbed away like an inflated plastic ball while I tried to sink efficiently. This time my brother Esmond wasn't there to save me. Young Socrates the coffee jerk had a seizure on the subway. He survived it. *Don't shake your infant ever, it might just perish.* In my dream, I chewed on broken glass, not some theory of propositions. Here is one: to blow it is black. Stalled at 14th St.-Union Square—though 14 is the year of disunion. I felt sorry for a little girl seated across from me. Then St. Augustine leapt in the garden and turned the page fervently. *Ladies and gentlemen, we are being held momentarily by the train's dispatcher, please be a sick and good patient like Hans of the lung. We should be moving shortly.* If you believe that, you are religious. Or gutsy. There was nobody to sue. Ads bled. Slouch of ignorance.

Hildegard the Unsteady

I didn't know I was going to be Hildegard, but then I was Hildegard.

I have visions, they are scientific of the ways of God. For instance, the toddlers' safety-orange doublets, which make them safe. Especially from doubts. Double + doubt = doublet. Every thought has its negation, which is its backside. My doublet was unsafety-yellow. I might be hit by a bright yellow taxi cab speeding.

You stole the safety-orange bit from another perception. No I didn't. Perceptions can be shared between individuals who are poems.

St. Hildegard believed in God, so she sang of him. I, Hildegard, sing of God so I will believe in Him.

A tan notebook entails tan hair, except that nobody has that. But they have tan skin. My hair is beige. I.e., light brown. Alright. My skin is pale like a bleached napkin. If I had used a black notebook, then my haircut would be black. But I might still be Hildegard.

Black icing means you are going to die. So I don't eat it.

In the snow, steps were taken.

It will snow on November 17th, I had a prophetic vision. I put my boots on to be ready.

Sure you can sit here.

What's going on?

Do you want that hot or iced?

To stay or to go?

With milk?

Gott-milk?

Hildegard is medium-tall and tan with bushy tan hair like a cardboard box turned into a character.

The napkin didn't work because I wiped my mouth on it.

Some people on seats sit straight, others curl like question marks with dots for feet. When they stand up, they become exclamation points. Defending convictions.

Hildegard made treatises, some were natural, some unnatural.

St. Hildegard drew treatises, composed drawings and deduced musics.

Black jeans which are new imply trying too hard.

Hildegard became a none at age 15, it was effortless. Then followed seventeen pages, then my visions began.

Hildegard saw a mail truck.

The spinning fans are enemy attempts to hypnotize you into detesting everything.

The antidote is to blink rapidly for three minutes. Whether three has to do with the holy trinity is uncertain.

I do not favor the number 3, I prefer 4 or 5, I am not saintly.

2 is also attractive. With angle and curve.

The *u* in *four* brings voluptuous pleasure.

Bells clattered.

I spied stretch marks that were luminous. My left hand uncurled gently.

The sunlight igniting the window blinds is not God. The world spoke French to thrust its tongue out at you.

That deaf, etc. kid sure plays a mean pinball.

I saw a young man with handwriting smaller than mine, it offended me. However, he used a pencil. I debated whether to copy him. He was blond and husky and wan.

My hand was messier, like bird scratches like snow, that way nobody could read it.

Your character is your will, you can shape it into an artwork or a mechanical procedure.

The flowers wore green plastic dresses on their stems, perhaps these were girdles. Proudly they held their heads up. Flowers are one example of an organic whole, which is the model for a beautiful artwork, according to Immanuel Kant.

Immanuel says God with us.

As for *Hildegard*, one element is battle, the second one is uncertain.

Mystery is desirable. Because it's like NoDoz.

A former diminutive becomes a name in its own right. For example, *Hilda*. But that is later.

Diminuendo is a musical imperative with subjective validity. It could be in a hymn for unprepared piano. Thus I would be Hildegard the Unready.

The adjectives were weaklings.

The clouds came in and took away the sentences. Leaving ideas of ideas.

Wait until this world leaves your head, whereupon another can arise there.

Plastic eyeglasses with thick black rims on a girl.

Ha ha ha ha.

Laughter peeled off the walls like green floral paper. Which, as a doodle, can be beautiful. See Kant's third *Critique*. The one about judgment and the creator.

Being an orphan, it was logical for her to love God the father.

Being an orphan, she entailed His non-existence.

Acting becomes impossible when there is an audience.

Writing is acting without an audience.

The fan blades picked up speed. A fan is like a flower.

But modes@God.disorg.

Vincent painted flowers.

St. Vincent is a name somebody else stole first. There were two who were different.

Yes, okay, that's what I'm saying.

I, Hildegard, tugged intently on one sideburn in my childhood.

Now it is impossible, wait until later, when Hildegard returns.

Faith is patience.

Being a patient is a virtue like manliness.

A man swept a sidewalk. He had arms and a blue cap. The dirt went into the gutter, where the street sweeper, a machine not a man, would brush it forward. Then where should it go?

I bruised my eyesight.

Twelve dollars. Newspaper. That's who he reminds me of.

Who is Hildegard? Hildegard is not yet a poet. Hildegard is meant to be a poet. Hildegard is inchoate.

I licked my tooth where it hurt, but I did not report my sensation to the audience.

This is too naive, it cannot last without becoming phony, unconvincing, boring.

My shirt sleeves were long yet immodest.

Hildegard saw a finger twirling a hair. She didn't own them.

Girls in school jumpers filed unevenly by the window.

A belt is for holding up trousers. What is Hildegard for?

*

I should be happy with the peace and birds, instead I feel tormented.

What the room writes is different from what the world writes, right now I am locked in.

I was going to be you or we, but I was not allowed to be. Hildegard is she, which is another possibility.

I wrote so as not to slide into the hole slowly opening in the boyish chest of the floor.

Too-bright window with television cables that the world could use to whip you.

Trees with green leafed-out branches trembling with a nervous energy.

I turned to face the corner, it is an architectural chill pill.

The thing to write in a room is about the neck knot or the eyelid twitch.

Spinoza says the mind only knows the body, it is the idea of it.

Everything had to pass through her nerves first, so it came out jangly or with static.

My elbows hurt from resting on the world's armrests. They are filthy as in movie theaters.

This Hildegard was an unblessed abyss.

St. Hildegard was the patron saint of rapid cyclers, manic depressives, coughers and vaporizers.

A vapor is a depressed or hysterical nervous condition.

Her treatises were confessions or exhortations. For example, no self-service or girl-on-girl action where one plays the man. Therefore she was sometimes near-sighted in visions. She also suffered from poor circulation, which causes extremities to fall asleep and be numb, later to awaken and tingle excitedly. Like a volume or a conundrum.

An asylum is a hackneyed solution. It's better to stay dizzy.

As with her idiolect mixing German, Latin and weird letters.

I am Hildegard von Dickon. I had hoped to become Mathilde, but I developed a case of Hildegard, which affected the prognosis for the war among my elements.

It will be a long wait with ersatz scaffolds.

People have lips, birds have beaks. I, Hildegard, have a book cover. It's hard and clothbound. Plus much more typing up to do, if I am to be heeded.

Subways boast infectious seats. I rubbed my jeans at the right inner thigh, it was anxious, not sexual.

A day stayed in bed but did not enjoy it.

First something else, then something else.

Hildegard decided that her illustrations were bad, therefore she was not William Blake, despite several counterarguments. A war occurred between his elements also. It was in black and white. They won't understand that.

Being a visionary requires seeing through the tawdry appearances. Therefore it is like being a philosopher.

Boredom summoned the sirens. Then we gave up, applied unguent of 55 SPF, slipped out of the immediate context.

Nothing good could come of *this*. So we sought *that*.

So so so. La la la. As in music.

Theory of demonstratives in De. Uncleaving.

Hildegard lived in a chapter which got inserted even though it was an excommunicate.

Daughter & Father

My father was a virgin, and I came to be in a virgin birth. I was born from his great fantasizing head. Or from his narrow Christlike rib cage. Or from his deep navel ringed with dark coarse hair. Or from his lush left armpit. Or from the dirt under his index fingernail. Or from his wagging, angled, unreliable but not yet totally hopeless prick.

Sleeping Beauty

Shall we love and forgive everyone? Shall we know that man is good and can be good, if properly guided?

I would rather keep on napping, thanks. Where is my baby blanket?

Do not try to kiss me.

Unrated

Within the privacy of her own room, Moira let go of life (it was uncut, life-size) and wiped the come off her fingers. *That*, at least, was not imaginary.

The Crumbs

Compassion

Listen, pigeon. I know you're bored and hungry and self-hating. I know you waddle around in a dusty feathery loneliness, clucking, disconsolate, revolted at all your peers in your peer group. I know you fly sometimes, but mostly look around for bread crumbs or puke to peck at. Transform yourself. Become a dove or a sparrow. A weed, a twig in the shade, a lusty imprecation. Just quit bugging me. I have better things to do than to care about you. I have my whole life to lead.

Good or Bad?

The older Chinese lady crinkled with plastic, read an English-language pamphlet with comic book-style illustrations. I lorded it over my bench. Spanish wafted over our matching brunette heads. Chinese lady, I salute you. My neck hurts. Sinners in orange Hi-Liter bibs sweep up leafy garbage. I had straight shoulders. Now I have a Mona Lisa smile, it plays like a dreamy kid around my lips. Tingling all over: o.d. to joy. Nerves are fantastic. But the tall beautiful white-haired lady I have known forever is dying. Passing go-go boots exclaimed it. The Chinese lady seemed sad, moved on after less than two minutes. Did I think the wrong thing? Somebody has to pay. Sh! Don't explain, just descry. I should've quit while I was a head, not a chest. Even the tweets of birds seem black in melancholy. Pink is a raincoat antidote on a pretty younger Chinese lady who sits down abruptly. I accidentally killed a tiny red bug on my composition book. I must perform penance. The Chinese girl laughs to herself in Chinese. Ideogram on margin. Check out the distant mountains. Bodega in the foreground. Unemployed scholar/hermit-fisherman wades through sea of traffic. Is loss more? Inkblot day.

Notions

To be a button and hold things together vs. to be a button hole trying to flap free: the older and younger sisters. The only child is a zipper. The adopted child is velcro. The twins are a snap.

Vagrant Wannabe

My keys pinched my flabby female hip. That's why it is bad to have a home.

Similitude (or, Argument by Analogy)

Oedipus is like Diogenes. No, Oedipus is like Lear. No, Oedipus is like Antigone. No, Antigone is like the Prodigal Daughter. No, the Prodigal Daughter is like Jephthah's Daughter. No, Jephthah's Daughter is like Ishmael. No, Ishmael is like the Princess and the Pea. No, the Princess is like Iphigenia. No, Iphigenia is like Electra. No, Electra is like Ophelia. No, Ophelia is like John the Baptist. No, John the Baptist is like the Holy Spirit. No, the Holy Spirit is like St. Francis. No, St. Francis is like Sir Franz. No, Sir Franz is like Antigone. No, Antigone is like Prince Søren. No, Prince Søren is like Kid Isaac. No, Kid Isaac is like Agnes, who is herself like Antigone.

One Reason To Be Self-Hung

Being spared. Do it, lamb.

Adoration of the Magi

In the fairy tale, the infant had an old man's face and was wise. He could bless and thereby save them. One fellow prayed, profile against halo, fingers almost touching the infant Jesus' pudgy left foot. Another looked down, holding his offering which

resembled a pastry. The third—the one in black with the tall hat—looked away, clutching his gift tightly. Guilt or doubt? But only *his* face was an echo in mood and angle of the infant's. As if he alone *also* saw the suffering ahead (i.e., to their right). Behind him, to his left, a shadowy dark figure, head bowed, servile, perhaps leaning on a crutch or holding the back of the Virgin's chair. Gentle lyrical figures on the other side of the Magi. Vertically bisecting the painting, a more everyday scene: one man gesturing with thumb, one raising a hand in surprise while on his other hand sits a bird (brownish-black and orange), two kids looking off (in boredom, not in knowing melancholy), and the horses. Two ribby dogs, one reddish-brown, one white, along the bottom edge. Sassetta should have painted one of the kids seeing and knowing, as I, Agatha, saw and knew, when I was 3. Now I am 11 and frightfully precocious. The sad Magus does look Russian; which one is he, Balthasar? That is one of my pet names. I have to go to lunch now with my Mama. Tuna fish sandwiches for both of us and a butterscotch sundae for myself alone. Schrafft's has old ladies.
They don't know about the power of *His* suffering extremities.

St. Minna

Wasn't I *supposed* to be a saint? That is why this life seems so wrong and clumsy. But I was too weak and selfish, I let God down. Now I inquire, Is it too late for me?

St. Minna sharing her tuna sandwich with a beggar. St. Minna giving her hoodie to a beggar (a poor knight).

St. Martin, St. Francis and St. Minna: each first experienced his calling while giving his cloak to a mendicant. The following night, each had a dream. One of Christ, another of a celestial palace. Minna dreamt of a divine tenement vestibule.

St. Minna heals the leg sores of a bum.

St. Minna cures the toothache of a geezer.

St. Minna stops the diarrhea of an infant.

I feel a new professional compulsion, a *Sturm und Drang* of spiritual activity. Watch for me on street corners, avenues, boulevards and arched bridges. You can recognize me by my long uncombed black hair and stringy bangs. Also by my limp, which, in its slow and rolling motion, is not unalluring to strangers, so I have heard. Not accidentally, *Minna* means love.

Interpretation of Italics

Italics can be deployed either to use a word emphatically or not to use it at all, i.e., merely to quote it or say something about it. Therefore italics represent the two purest spiritual modes: fervor and detachment.

However, the use of italics for a title suggests a third spiritual mode: invention. Is that the divinely impure mode?

Strategy

Hide. Hide in your room. Don't let them discover you. Turn into a strand of coppery brown hair and lie on the floor amid other snippets, dust and dirt. How could they single you out?

This place is disgusting, a sty.

Look for the copper lining. The frayed brown lining of your plaid jacket, with the soft strands waving from its cuff like the hair of a child or an old lady.

The young mothers take their children to school. I, Minna, sit on a bench, stupefied by leaves. A flying pigeon almost smacks into my forehead.

I dislike children. Unless I am one; then I like one.

Incidentally, *Minna* means diminutive will helmet. When it doesn't mean love.

II. DEVIATIONS

The Agnes Splinters

1 Agnes was a girl and crunch of leaves and missed her bedroom.

2 He went with bad men. Bandits.

3 The composition books have a black-and-white splatter pattern. One hundred sheets. Then the binding peeled off.

4 Twenty eiderdowns plus twenty mattresses equals forty days. But they are insufficient, like fairy tales.

5 How everything moves now!

6 Agnes was before with timbrels.

7 Once the daughter was Agnes, then Agnes was not the daughter.

8 We are Agnes.

9 Holes in the ribbon from not moving, being repeatedly struck.

10 Now go back the other way.

11 Metal wafers.

12 Silver as color and metal.

13 A cell is a possible object of experience, does that mean of knowledge?

14 Inside the room, she wailed up and down the mountain.

15 Mountain of sheets of paper, as if ripped from a book.

16   Because I don't know or because there is nothing to know. Beware of the red table, it wants to destroy you.

17   The red table has a silver edge and legs, but aluminum.

18   A thing can be lightweight or heavy.

19   E.g., a story, a blanket, a sheet of typing bond.

20   Stay in your room where there are no tables, *a fortiori* no red tables. Still the images of things stream by. They can't be forgiven but want to be forgiven. In that they are like you.

21   Metal discs.

22   Timbrel equals tambourine. Small hand drum with loose round metal plates.

23   To get a sound, shake or strike with the hand.

24   Perhaps aggressive. Violent.

25   The Partridge Family performed on television in the early 1970s.

26   Agnes was in the early 1970s, he went like Jephthah.

27   Girls can be loose.

28   Agnes Doran.

29   Different abbreviations with different meanings. AD vs. Ag.

30   A partridge not aggressive.

31   A partridge a bird to be sighted and killed, even though it has a song.

32   E.g., 'I Think I Love You.'

33   Was there a little girl, and what did she do? Was she the one who shook the tambourine? That one was boring.

34   Unclear name shrieked in the street, over and over, same note and intonation. It's distracting. I am trying to be Agnes.

35   I thought about being Agatha, but a timbrel is not a bell.

36   Bell-shaped breasts on silver platter, she is arguably the patron saint of bell-founders.

37   Then they fondled them. Or would. That is only in conviction.

38   It's no sin to fondle sentences.

39   A bedtime theory.

40   Bedroom I's. The knowing subject.

41   There was once a maiden who lived with her papa. He was an outlaw. He was in judgments.

42   Agnes and Jeffrey Doran.

43   I miss my bedroom.

44   While the papa was away, the girl became a musician. But then he returned.

45   Then she fondled them. Or would. But he returned then.

46   *Do not enter,* said the doily on the floor. Men with floral designs upon the father. Aka the papa. Aka Papa.

47   Or upon the daughter.

48   Crunch of paper.

49   The lines aren't straight anymore, it takes longer.

50   Angular form of frequency. Up and down the bedroom.

51   I.e., mountain.

52   Then the floor tipped suddenly, she slid into the corner by the window.

53   Then the furniture slammed into me. By striking.

54   Jingling.

55   Jingle does not equal jangle. One high and light, the other harsh and discordant.

56   Short verse or tune with catchy repetition.

57   Series of clinking or tinkling sounds.

58   Timbre of girl and composition notebook.

59   Chimed. As in chimed in.

60   Fell, as in fell out.

61   The entailment of Agnes.

The Scrapped Book of Minna Maude Ingvar

Rue, Tourette's

The city where you come to leave *I thought*: I saw it die. Tall young man with a shaved head indicating gullibility, not radiation. Brown shirt for UPS or picking up coy signals. Or some historical unsayable. Punctuation a spiritual question not yet answered honestly. Leaves of inference. Faces tilt like pinball machines. Cursive cursing. God's a cursor.

If you're too something, the smell of dread will get you. Bus shelter cries, broken glass. Flushed table. The *I fell*, towering, tapered to pointlessness vs. the awesome awful. Damian the twin of Cosmas, *Damian* means tame, *Cosmas* means order, ornament, beauty. Is that sinful? Tower Records went out of business, Anton Webern's notes were not recoverable.

It's easier to write if you have nothing to say. Fucking cunthole asshole thermometer bastard emergency exist sign. I meant exit. Came, saw, crawled away. Infant in a stroller. Can an infant fake its bile? Lie down in the crib, birds flap by with wires, the world coughs nervously. Tics developed.

Metropolitan Lyric

Buying sunglasses. Throwing away philosophy. Almost impossible not to deal with a shadow.

Only children and their accompaniments allowed in the playground.

Yellow taxi yields the fantasy of escape, e.g., to Bergdorf's. A good man? Boots with heels to change the whole reality. One page isn't enough, but lack of concision is ugly. Songs in a bright grey which hurts. So hide out. However, there are fisticuffs with shouts inside my cell. If a girl screams in her head, does it fall off because she hears it? Get up and go. The capitalized *G* can't help but be inspiring. But I am light-intolerant.

Rub your own face fondly. Face another direction. I collided with a Frau named Inge. She was sharp yet kind. I ran away from her forever. My room has dandruff. A dog barks, plagiarizing another dog. Beware of whining. Seizure day. Epileptic, Tourettic, operatic, or etc. It could ruin balance. A baseball cap is one kind of helmet which many of us wear. Loss Mets.

It's Better to Wait Mutely (or, Hit the Mute)

I lived in a room that trembled. A rounded belly of a Lucas Cranach Eve came into my vision. I lived in a room that trembled, in a building that trembled. Unpredictably. My room shuddered with anxiety or dismay, not acceleration.

A book was beige, a man's mouth was crooked, an old lady yammered just outside the door.

The silence before the great building falls is not like the silence after it falls, because that latter silence never gets broken. Secrets as proofs of life. Something must be hidden. A leaf hid her labia majora, but where was her bush? Pubic hair another consequence of the fall. Adam and Eve were both redheads, or else Adam was a redhead, Eve a blonde, or else Adam was a redhead, Eve a brunette. Amschel was a brunet. Eve and Adam waited for God to collapse mentally. Moses waited for the burning bush to crumble. I, Minna, waited for the fortress to topple. Too impatient to bring a scene to life, she chewed on slivers. Intersubjectivity's overcrowded. I still have a narrow medieval pot belly. Op. cit.

I lay on the wooden floor. It had knots. I don't know anybody. Plastic bags rustle with prophecies. Knees bend if you are still a young woman. Is Minna? Minna is Minna Maude Ingvar. Holes in sweaters and reasonings. What if I am afraid to be alone? A tooth aching with compassion. Baby or wisdom? Goodness is available to many, if not to all. A bearded man says he hears voices, one tells him to kill himself, he would never listen to it. A sullen guy left his ass at home, in his other jeans. Olive-green wool cap. Soul patch vs. knee patch. Or elbow. Then the paragraph heard a voice, it said, *Kill yourself!* The paragraph listened.

Look, Don't Sink

Cantilevered fellow-feeling. Discrete communiqués. A gorgeous ceiling with blades of grass.

My interior got mistaken for Grand Central Station. Trains ride into me which may or may not be subways. The underground Minna soiled herself whenever possible. Clack click cluck. Nothing has to do with everything. Something with nothing. The number 7. I like the short thick ones, she likes the tall skinny ones. But this I is Minna. Tryst in a hardware store, amidst steel wool and masking tape. Is he Chinese or Mexican? I dunno, does it matter? Yeah. He has a ponytail. Skintight mystery. Went so far inside me that he ended up in Philadelphia. Stupid! Away from shiny fixtures. Freedom is removing the splinter. Or mote? Or motet or mortal. Mort, Morty, Morton. Felled man. By roared shock test. *The Minna Splinters. The Minna Shards. The Minna Shreds. The Minna Morsels.* Sky as childhood vs. as cataract. Don't look down and you won't fall: cartoon dictum. I shouldn't be here. But they stared at me, so I remained to lick stamps.

Epistemology of Hairlines—No, False Alarm

The thing about the faces is so beautiful that I cannot write anything about faces. Next logical choice is backs of heads. Abruptly, my tenderness quits. In the café, an older man—glasses, dark baseball cap—picking his nose Hercules-style. Disgust and shame rushed my order, he muttered a soliloquy. In another possible world, I preached the ascension of sugar. Here, I hoarded milk and Reese's Pieces. Green. Or red like the rubber ball in bombardment. Huh? Having the sounds scolded out of you, it is hard not to be hard of hearing. I no longer allow them to use a razor on the back of my neck. I do not love myself. Nor Hercules' ersatz. Once I knew how to hear, then hit a silence. It pertains only to me, is my invention. Thin undergarments. Unprotected *x*. Flickers of darkness. Under pressure, a bell cracks. Call me Gershom. That's not her name, it is Minna Maude Ingvar. Nerve impulses rest for two measures. Stupor sonic. I am late for my epiphany, it won't wait. *Ha ha*, chortled the street below. They are shoveling away connectives such as *and* and *or*. Subatomic sentences wander. While I keep adding on, building, only to end up with a hollow tautology. The clang gives me away. *Ach nein*, that must be the shovel. Don't confuse logic with music, even though both end with *ic*. Ick or *ich*? But those, in contrast, *are* the same. Quit being such a knee jerk, Minna. Music broke its own rules. Logic was broken with its.

I Am Afraid Also

The fear of Mallevue hospital is available for two dollars and a window seat. Although it started in a different manuscript or street. Fear is contagious. *Malle* – *l* + *t* = *Malte*. Nominal mathematics. L = love, t = truth. Mal = a time (as in one time, two times, etc.) or an illness or a badness. *Malle* – *am* + *be* = *Belle*. Spiritual aesthetics. I lied, the fear is inherited like a nobleman's title. Rue of martyrs, rule of cities: I see the mad ones gobbling crumbs. So this is a bed to die in. I would have thought it was one you could lie in, aka make up.

Once Minna wrote a pamphlet called *His Head Is Their Hotel, His* meaning God's. That was when she believed it. Fierce blue eyes like a husky's: the tall man growled at her, panted. A bell went off. Am I dead yet? Minna Gershom. Gershom Minna. The I has its attributes, of which we know only two, though there are infinitely many. A small room laughed, flung its arm around the patient. Patronizing, not fraternizing. No consolation in barred windows. To go mad here and die to this world—would that be so terrible? Would the terror be forgotten, or be beautiful? Even a beatitude?

But the people—she saw the prosaically broken. Flea-bag, SRO, émigré: halfway house, halfway prison. Inverse luxury. Like this, you could ride the public transportation of language, forget to inspect and honor your shreds. An elegant carriage-house restaurant is a relic, a paper plate is *au courant*. They cast you out, say, *We'll find other demons*. A bus breathed heavily like a fat man and lumbered off, crowded. You: too thin to offer seats. It's time to move. At lunch all gather in the cafeteria for knishes, pickles. Yet isn't food an offense?

Vacancy

His head is their hotel. Her head is not their hotel, since she won't let them die in it. His head is the Godhead, Minna does a head fake, foils herself. Throat-clearer ate a bagel slowly. Badly dressed woman expectorated. Threat-clearer whistled. I serenade gutters, they rebuff my retreats. Dignity has to do with deep breaths, not a chest that is sunken. Minna ruined the pure pullover by stabbing its sleeve with her razor-sharp pen. Only a paper clip could hold me together, but it slid off the table in protest. The cars are dying. Something wrong with my eardrum, it gets agitated, vibrates with other ambitions. Sonata for bottle scavenger. I discarded my high-school sweatshirt, my gaiters. Found words that were the wrong shape for my mouth. Its narrow palate.

One way to go that would not follow logically from the illness: to fall upon the sharp number 7 already mentioned. The sanatorium in my head has 800 beds for the thoughts to lie down in and perish. A true poet wears a stanza, but I lack gratitude. Lacy brassiere, young man's briefs. Paper clip accused you. Refused to help. Snotty silver. Dusk approached like the landlord. A shout, a scrape, a scrap of experience—either internal (subject) or external (object), that depends on its dysfunction. The world might be tight in the shoulders. The day's death could leap out of the sidewalk trash can. A corner of *The Idiot* detached itself and hurled itself to the floor to join the paper clip. In protest like consumption, doubt or Franz K. The idea of interesting as a condiment. Of boring as a station. Of thrilling as an indent. The black lacquered master of the book. A knight of grooved, circular phrases. Where skip = stick. Needles have knees.

First Person of Truth

@ 6:08   The liar is a sentence that secretly commits suicide.

@ 6:09   In asserting its falsity, the liar becomes a self-destroyer and a sentential rebel. That is true.

@ 6:11   There was a man who had two sons, the younger and favorite was a daughter. And she said to him, *Give me my share of your living*. And he complied. A few days later, the daughter gathered or else lost her wits and left. But not forever.

@ 6:13   They instructed me when I returned here to keep a diary—it might help me to recover. In truth, they plan to steal it to use as proof of their theory, so they can banish me to a mental sanatorium which I will detest, cf. Friedrich Nietzsche.

@ 6:14   First Basel, then Jena. Even though strictly, university ≠ asylum. That is an analytic non-identity statement. Not all institutions are the same.

@ 6:15   For one thing, they have different colored walls.

@ 6:16   He, Friedrich Nietzsche, was 44 when he went to Basel Klinik, whereas I, Mia Dickey, was 41 when I came to Melville Hostel. Unless I was 14. In logic, *unless* amounts to *or* (via *if not* . . . , *then* . . .), symbolized by v.

@ 6:17   I was allowed in because I *seem* to be a 14-year-old. Nobody really knows me.

@ 6:18   The logical *or* is inclusive, the existential *or* is exclusive. If logical, then inclusive, therefore, by contraposition, if exclusive (i.e., not inclusive) then not logical. The *or* pertaining to life or living is illogical. But sharp, not dull. That is true. To spurn the advances of dilemmas is stupid.

@ 6:19   Italics are used for scare quotes or for emphasis. You might emphasize a fear with them. Such as the fear of amounting to something. Or the fear of not.

@ 6:21   Scare quotes are used for names or to hold something away from you, e.g., in doubt or mockery. Perhaps due to dread.

@ 6:23   Doubts can snowball.

@ 6:24   Ultimately, doubts and snowballs will hit walls.

@ 6:26   Here, the walls are neither snow-white nor Snow White; nevertheless, snow is white. So 'Snow is white' is true—for example, on mountains in Switzerland. In contrast, on *my* mountain, snow was often grey or yellow. Due to accidents, not to its essence; regardless, *there* snow was grey.

@ 6:28   'Snow White' is true iff (if and only if) Snow White. Never mind that Snow White is not a sentence. What is truth? My Pilot pen asks that. I feel thirsty.

@ 6:31   The liar sentence has a will to death—but to being dead already, not to dying. In calling itself false, it is trying entirely to undo itself as a claim. However, it fails at that. It becomes a contradiction instead.

@ 6:32   There exists no liar paradox. Strictly speaking.

@ 6:33   The liar appears to be simple self-denial, but suicide is always also self-assertion. The liar's suicide *requires* its assertion. It is an impure, therefore a failed, ascetic.

@ 6:34   That failure has everything to do with the absurdity of truth. With its being first person singular, aka subjective.

@ 6:35   The truth as first-personal. Find a way to think that *one* thought.

@ 6:36   That *one* thought is your fate. Ineluctable vocation.

@ 6:37   All ascetics are impure and fail—they *want* to deny themselves.

@ 6:39   All skeptics are impure and fail—their fear does not protect them. *Aren't you one of his disciples?* No, not I, that must be another! Thereby you fulfill *his* prophecy, are a loyal disciple despite yourself. How much better to be faithful willingly. Even if *he* is a paradox and moreover gives offense. *He* meaning just: the truth. *He* being figurative.

@ 6:41   Fears can snowball.

@ 6:43   I am the truth. The I = the truth. That is the philosophical. Not merely the spiritual.

@ 6:44   You could be too weak or stupid or craven for the philosophical. Because it says, You, be an outcast!

@ 6:47   Friedrich Nietzsche swept the paths of the garden of the psychiatric asylum where he resided, Ludwig Wittgenstein swept the paths of the garden of the monastery where he boarded, and I, Mia Dickey, shall sweep the paths of the garden of the home for wayward girls where I lodge like a bit of apple stuck in the throat. These gardens are not Edens. That is true if and only if these gardens are not Edens.

@ 6:49   The snake, the maiden, the trees, the expulsion. All true. But not the explanation.

@ 6:51   The truth is first-personal. That is lived, not judged. As judged, it's incompleteness. Not all truths are judgeable. I am the truth ≠ I am true.

@ 6:53   Likewise, not all falsehoods are judgeable. In calling itself false, the liar indirectly judges itself doubly.

@ 6:54   The standard reading of the liar is that it judges itself singly—as false. Thus if it's false, it's true, and if it's true, it's false. But that leads to contradiction. So the liar *entails* a contradiction without itself *asserting* a contradiction. But that reading is wrong.

@ 6:55   Instead, the liar contradicts itself: it *says* that it is and isn't false—because it says, 'This sentence is false' and "'This sentence is false' is false'. (Or, 'I am false' and "'I am false' is false'.) Since it *asserts* a contradiction, it is simply false. Its falsity cannot make it true. No paradoxical looping occurs. The grand paradox was a sham.

@ 6:57   Whereas the so-to-speak first person paradox, the paradox of subjectivity, i.e., of truth, which is the *true* paradox—

@ 6:58   But does the liar really *say* in part "'This sentence is false' is false'? And even if it says that, does 'is false' equal 'is not the case', i.e., 'not'? The logicians present it thus, but *they* can be terribly crude.

@ 6:59   Saying a sentence is true is synonymous with saying that the sentence says something that is so. Saying it's false is synonymous with saying that it says something that isn't so. 'Is false' doesn't equal 'is not the case' but it includes it: 'N' is false = 'N' says something (namely, that N) that is not so.

@ 7:00   Therein the simple, intuitive idea behind correspondence. A semantic gloss rather than an absolute realist metaphysical postulate. The symbolization of falsehood by mere negation in extensional logic is thus acceptable. If any simplification is.

@ 7:01   What of the special reflexive content of the liar and *its* symbolization?

@ 7:02   The liar is 'This sentence is false', so the term 'this sentence' refers to 'This sentence is false'; it speaks of that sentence. So doesn't what it *says* amount to: This sentence (it) is false and 'This sentence is false' is false?

@ 7:03   But now the two claims of falsehood seem identical, so where is the contradiction? Relatedly, the logicians symbolize the liar simply by $\neg L$.

@ 7:04   Back to the smooth ground! In the winter, they let us go ice-skating. My ankles are weak, they wobble and bend inwards. My white skates are scuffed and so tight! Or was that in the past?

@ 7:05   No, there *is* a contradiction, the iterated predicate creates it! The dream of pure negation has to be relinquished. Like that of pure doubt. Naysayer's fairy tales.

@ 7:07   Once Mia Dickey was 9 years old: compulsively, she read fairy tales. The homophone *Nein* means no in German. Much brilliant philosophy, fiction and poetry have been written in German. Robert, Ludwig, Friedrich, Friedrich, and Friedrich, for example. Tall mountains speak German. I ran away to them. True, true, true, true and true.

@ 7:08   It's true that *Robert* means bright fame, *Ludwig* means famous warrior, and *Friedrich* means peace ruler. They're in German. What *Mia* means is still contested; the options are wished-for child, rebellion and my. Not in German. But *Mia* = *Minna* by double negation: $nn Mia$, $\neg\neg Mia$. So in German, other options exist.

@ 7:09   Ludwig and Friedrich should have had each other's names. They are not intersubstitutable *salva veritate*.

@ 7:10   I am terribly thirsty. Nevertheless, I don't eat dirty snow.

@ 7:12   The liar has everyone fooled. Then a revision of classical logic could flaunt its attractions. But we stop short of that, cite plain contradiction. We who? The royal we, not the common one. Still a mouthpiece for truth. Of course I am somebody. Or other. For instance, Mia Dickey.

@ 7:13   I am a real somebody. Yet also a nobody. Don't call me MD as in SK, LW, BS, FN. Metaphysician, heal thyself! The others wished to provoke a few choice readers; I don't want to move even one reject. Is that selfishness or humility? Pride or feminine chastity? The Sienese Sassetta painted St. Francis to resemble a maiden who stood boldly naked yet demure before the disapproving father when Francis renounced the father's lucrative way of life for a life of the soul.

@ 7:14   Ah, Mia. That's for the birds!

@ 7:15   Do you hear me giggling? Will you join in? Those with ears to hear—

@ 7:15   *No! Not until you prove to us that—*

@ 7:15   I didn't think so.

@ 7:16   *They* steal this notebook, want to play interlocutor. But *I* am my true interlocutor. They don't understand me.

@ 7:17   Ludwig and Friedrich left scraps which the others arranged to create a thought sequence and *Nachlass*. Who shall figure out the order and connection of my unruly notes?

@ 7:20   The presenting of itself as true is the form of existence of the assertoric sentence—its mode of life. The way it *has* life. The liar is such a sentence; it presents itself as true. Thus its form belies its content. It can't transcend itself in action. (Questions, exclamations, and commands have other forms.) Form = way of acting.

@ 7:21   The fantasy of pure transcendence has to be dropped. Pure as in absolute.

@ 7:22   The word *is* life. Life = word = truth: there is a philosophical meaning to that. It is no fairy tale, or else some fairy tales are also *true*.

@ 7:23   Fairy tales can elicit philosophizing—wonder.

@ 7:24   How are fictions or fantasies true? Oh, don't pursue that question now, it is a distraction.

@ 7:26   Given that truth is life and falsehood is death, the liar aims to present itself as dead, by saying it is so. It is trying to be honest. Yet to do that, it has simultaneously to manifest itself as alive—just by making an assertion. Which latter it needs to do to slay itself. The combination leads to its *stating* that it is alive (true). Contradiction!

@ 7:27   The liar negates itself, but any negation is a negative *assertion*. Formally, it shows faith in itself.

@ 7:28   If I think, then I am true! I cannot judge myself out of truth in the sense of existence, i.e., reality. And in the other sense, agreement with reality? Here hides a connection.

@ 7:28   The I might be a person or thought or sentence. Regardless, it's impossible for me to judge sincerely and not be truthful.

@ 7:29   Truth has two meanings: fidelity and reality.

@ 7:30   The hidden connection *is* best?

@ 7:31   Harry Clyde has short bushy red hair. I, Mia Dickey, have long wavy black hair. That much is true. Harry Clyde is my favorite orderly.

@ 7:32   Says who? Say I, of course. Every sentence is *formally* first person singular.

@ 7:33   Now it's time for the breakfast of porridge and coffee, you must descend to the dining hall. Say I, not Harry; he's down in the common room with the others. True.

@ 7:34   Lunatics talk to themselves, they say *you*. Do we need the universal or the existential quantifier to symbolize the preceding sentence? Upside-down A vs. backwards E: ∀ vs. ∃. 'Flipping equals flipping' is a logical truth. The genius Descartes invented the ex- and why-axes, over which flipping occurs.

@ 7:35   He was austere and supposedly denied everything to be reborn as the I, a thinking thing. Only he didn't. Our modern father.

@ 7:36   It's fine to go to the sink, wash your hands of your mundane self—but there's a residue.

@ 7:37   What is the I? Does thinking truly need it? What is thinking? Does the I truly need it?

@ 7:39   René Descartes plotted his escape from himself with his first clear and distinct point, in the new mathematics. A sloping line from the origin (0,0). Necessarily, he was alone—except for God, his function. Solitary confinement is good. Otherwise, institutions are distractions and unpersuasive. They have to be left.

@ 7:41   I know because I did it once upon a time. Knowledge by affliction qua knowledge by defection. At the start of the different *Wanderjahr*. A dark wood. Then a valley, not a mountain: invert the acute angle, i.e., the figure. Inter all hap, ye who abandoned there.

@ 7:42   Whereof Mia cannot speak, thereof shall she stay silent.

@ 7:43   Mia the wretch.

@ 7:45   Later, I returned of my own volition, not expecting to be incarcerated. Thought my robe would be the best robe—royal violet and silken, no bleached polyester bathrobe. To rematriculate can be a mistake, if not a mental disturbance. Is all of this mere prophecy of, e.g., Mallevue Hospital? From there, one could see ugly Queens.

@ 7:46   To return to where you are vs. to where you once were: these are philosophically different.

@ 7:47   *Our* home is Melville Hostel, hostel of the estate of the industrious one. My room is on a high floor—garret or closet or aerie. Someday my future self—dub it, say, Mina—might forswear that. Then will it still be true? Whom are you asking? Furthermore, my room is perched on a high mountain, the floor of my room is snow-covered. My footsteps crunch. That is true in poetry. But you will be late for breakfast. It should be possible to quit. Reach the full stop.

@ 7:48   How am I like a sentence?

@ 7:49   How am I like the truth?

*

@ 10:28   0, 1, 2 and 8 are metaphysical digits. Especially 0, which appears in the moment. Marry, a null. The once and future ring, say I, Mia. The starting bell for class. I hid in my wardrobe. It's infinitely devisable. Narnia? Austria? Biel? Thuringia? Actors have wardrobes, so do passers. Along great mountains. Inactors have wardrobes, too. And psyche wards, i.e., wards of the mental states, have robes. It's hard not to act at all. It's easier to act crazy.

@ 10:29   Yet Waldau ≠ Herisau, as demonstrated Robert Walser. Not all sanatoria are kindred. Actually, it was Robert who swept the paths. Friedrich only rudely flung leaves upon them.

@ 10:30   One day Robert fled to a wood, lay on his back in the snow, made a snow angel and died. Robert was a childlike old man. That is some of what is the case.

@ 10:31   Or else he lay on his side in the snow, became his own odd dead letter and quit being true. To quit having sense wasn't enough.

@ 10:34   The equation is not of sense, i.e., meaning with life, it's of truth with life. But then, what is meaning? My Razor Point pen pricks me like conscience or consciousness. Never mind! Stick to truth.

@ 10:39   Humans are like sentences. I must be loyal to the truth. Even naysayers, dissemblers, fantasizers, jokers and doubters adhere to some truths. Therefore to *the* truth.

@ 10:39   Furthermore, *from the inside*, any world is veridical. Look at make believe.

@ 10:41   The truth is enormous. What if it itself is contradictory? Harry Clyde tosses off contradictions while carrying trays of lunch to the bedridden girls. Or at least, seeming contradictions.

@ 10:41   Please, Mia, focus!

@ 10:42   There was a man who had two sons, the younger was a restless daughter. One day she demanded her share of the good and fled, apparently to engage in riotous living. In other words, she lay around, daydreaming. Is that different or the same?

@ 10:45   As for the liar, it would prefer not to.

@ 10:45   In the end, there *was* a Bartle in the box. How piteous.

@ 10:46   Friedrich said, *Eschew pity. Including self-pity. Pity is a pity.* However, I rebelled.

@ 10:48   The liar goes beyond nonsense. Nonsense is mere escapism. Sentences like grammar school pupils at play time. Vs. suicide.

@ 10:50   Some argue that the liar asserts nothing, it is absurd nonsense, neither true nor false. I, Mia, say the liar asserts too much—because it denies too much.

It denies itself altogether. It's different from other contradictions—maybe even absurd. Still, it's false, not nonsensical—

@ 10:51   But wait. The liar says, I am false, thus, 'I am false' is false. But if 'I am false' actually means, I am false and 'I am false' is false, then in calling itself false, the liar is further calling that covert contradiction false, thus negating itself again. But then it is also calling that second contradiction false, etc., *ad absurdum*. Doesn't that mean the liar has no stable meaning, it's funhouse nonsense?

@ 10:52   Hall of mirrors semantics—a weird idea. We could try mathematical induction to fix the liar's meaning. Still the infinite regress seems disturbing.

@ 10:54   Snake swallowing its own tale—infinity a vicious circle or a loopy narrative. Perhaps obsessing over the liar is itself a vice—and a mental illness. Instead, choose impassivity over wonder. Choose passivity. What if you can't?

@ 10:56   The answer's simple! The liar's subcontent cannot be put into its surface content to get an infinite regress. It doesn't belong there. The predicate 'is false' applies only to the liar, the lone referent of 'This sentence'—i.e., 'This sentence is false'. So the liar isn't meaningless, it's just false.

@ 10:57   Fine, but now, how is it true, i.e., alive, i.e., an assertion?

@ 10:58   Not all assertions end up true, yet each assertion *takes itself* for true—even the liar. This truthfulness is shown in its *action*, which is disguised by its content.

@ 10:58   Truth is form. It's *a priori*. But only for the first person singular.

@ 10:59   The truth shows itself. The buried I. Yes of assertions. What kind of truth is that?

@ 10:59   Taking oneself for true is the form. Truthfulness, sincerity.

@ 11:00   Is that equal to subjective truth? And is *that* equal to truth *simplicitur*?

@ 11:01   The assertoric way of life—its form—is truth. Yet truth is mortal.

@ 11:02   Standard contradiction a reckless accidental death. Simple falsehood a natural death. Suicidal paradox—pseudo-paradox—a premature death. Only the true paradox lives onward.

@ 11:03   Something wrong with this idea of life and death. Think harder.

@ 11:05   Anyway, what will happen to Tarski's truth schema "P is true' iff P' if the liar qua P has a second, buried clause, namely that it's false that it's false? For then the truth condition isn't on the surface. Must we give up the schema? *Ach, weh!*

@ 11:06   Don't get ahead of yourself, Mia. Go slow. The snow is too bright.

@ 11:06   Impatience the only sin? Franz Kafka said that. What if it's the only way to attain truth, i.e., salvation? Yea, impulsive is the truth. Also convulsive. It shocks head and world back to life, while waiting only enervates. Franz was a disinclined Kopfka who lay on his desk and dreamed.

@ 11:07   Although, didn't that dream already make another world? It could not help it. Meanwhile, Franz admired Robert. They shared a dreamy lanky sympathy.

@ 11:08   Beware of poetic syntax. The philosophers don't like it. You must be no philosopher.

@ 11:09   Beware of spiritual semantics. The philosophers—well, so what? Perhaps truth doesn't like the philosophers. The philosopher-kings, anyway. It prefers the philosopher-princes: eager poets, fearless outcasts, noble strumpets. Quixotic knights.

@ 11:10   Logos said, Be Ishmaels. Here is a hand, it is raised against dumb Everyman.

@ 11:11   It said, The way up and down is wonder and pain. Truth wrestles with itself.

@ 11:13   Harry Clyde said the soul's report is fantastically, even impossibly deep. Mia Dickey says the life of the mind demands keen spontaneity.

@ 11:14   Therefore try to be acutely sensitive and vulnerable. It's better to feel thoughts than to doubt them. Life is truth, assertion a form of adoration.

@ 11:15   Once a girl thought so much, her thoughts were very sensitive. Like the princess bruised by the P buried under the twenty mattresses and twenty eiderdowns. P is for proposition. Then she, Mia Dickey, ran away like Søren Kierkegaard and remained a bachelor. No, she, Mia, stayed and married the world, even though it was huge and it hurt.

@ 11:17   Thus groan, think, look—here in the leaf-strewn garden. The maiden with the red sores on her scrawny legs, my fellow inmate: true and indubitable. I know we are in pain. I feel it, believe it, think it. Some thoughts demand empirical imagination.

@ 11:19   Other thoughts demand philosophical consternation. The first person singular form of truth, as confessed by the liar, is such a thought—

@ 11:19   Right then I saw him: the gangly man with the flashing yellow crest. He moved toward me with awkward eagerness. He was no mime—he could not even perform the action he was doing, it ran away from him. I, too, failed my first and only acting audition. Everything stayed hidden. What cannot be shown must be scribbled down. His name was Robert Wallis. He gave an earnest yet arrogant bow. Wore a strange buckled outfit suitable for long walks through block letters of city streets, cursives of forests.

@ 11:21   Thin and fictional, he smiled as he recited my own prose poem: The next messiah shall be an actor playing all the heroic outcast roles, thereby suffering for our sins, with joyous pained eyes and a gaunt strong tender face like that of Vanessa Redgrave. Like Robert Walser, that lady was tall, thin, noble, and craved ardently to feel things. Like Friedrich Nietzsche, this girl is short, thin, noble, and wants fervently to feel thoughts. The actor as chosen one shall perish walking in the woods, first making bird scratch handwriting with this wandering, finally lying face down on the snowy hill in Central Park to become a *sui generis* punctuation mark. Her name, too, shall be Robert—i.e., bright fame. Which was to be my name instead of Mia, had I been born a boy. Snow as sparkling gems, trees as fine medieval damsels, kids' snow suits as colorful banners in life's procession. Hear the doves cooing, the sparrows chirping. Birds chirp like excitable maidens. A greenish-yellow canary flies into a mine to trill coal into diamonds. Streets yield embers or fuels for an Überfinch. Once a great aspect was dawning. It halted. Fly away from the bad apple danish, gloom will stick in your throat. World a nil wafer promising resurrection and communion. Where is my rucksack, it is under my big eyes, it needs mending. Suicide under the left eye, madness under the right eye, now blink the sanatorium into a castle alias monastery. A sensitive lineage allows exactly you to be the world's beloved, let all of it fondle you. But I am my world: the idiocosm! I am its Word, the idiolect. Narcissus the solipsist is performed by the I in his bubble bath. The thought bubble is a worry. No it's not! The value is Life, the word is World, the loved is Beautiful and True and Lovely. So sang one who was personality-wise akin to a mischievous thrush and a Medieval robber *cum* hood. Who stole away from the rich to gab as the poor. Dub him Robin for three seconds. He gave voice to my lyric of yore, when I was, say, Minna Dickey—a small, somewhat orange European bird or else Dark-Aged and a thief. O *or of my possibility*—

@ 11:25   All of a sudden the dead earnest adult Ricardo appeared outside the small window on the door—there is no privacy, it has been disproven—and yelled, *What is this, you lyrical slackers? Such dereliction! It's time for stringent meditations, discourses methodical not fanciful.* He was dressed rigorously, a madness scientist in a White-Out laboratory coat. Feared disorderly mental conduct. Relatedly, he was an agoraphobe, although earlier he had been a claustrophobe. *Stop hiding your eyes*, he scolded, *we are not playing games such as Blind Girl's Bluff, this playpen is the wrong slope. Reason is a linear function.* Then peace in the beaks of pigeons by way of truth-tree branches fluttered off. In me, no more roles of knights, actors, bawds or giants. Good tidings appeared probably grim. Fear, hunger and the lost way lay ahead. I, Mia Dickey, was cursed with my own philosophical company. The mountain resembled a proof instead of a verse.

@ 11:27   Fling yourself off of it? It off of you? Sheer temptation.

@ 11:28   The pure one stops writing to go mad or silent.

@ 11:29   The impure one goes mad to keep writing, keeps writing to go mad—

Philosophical Scrap

1   Therefore yellow.

2   Origami canary.

3   I was dying from unbreathable air. Or hot air.

4   Elevators vs. birds. Childhood got stuck. That's another inkpad.

5   Brown ≠ yellow.

6   The maroon jacket plummeted. Unless it was brown with white piping. It swished, it didn't pipe like a bird or Franz.

7   This is Siegfried, do you have a room with a piano today?

8   A theory. A tune. An apology. A zipper.

9   Straight thick eyebrows like zippers. I zipped my forehead to my eye sockets, everybody was relieved.

10 Mona Lisa once had eyebrows. Let us mourn them.

11 They were curved like Romanesque arches, mine are pointed like Gothic arches. They were raised in skepticism, which is a facial disorder like a smile or grimace.

12 I just lied, my eyebrows are straight like sticks of licorice. They are used to scowl.

13 Don't put everything in your mouth. Why not? I coughed up a hairball of world. That's another mousepad.

14   Could an infant fake a scowl?

15   Could an adolescent fake a pimple?

16   If I were still cool, I would have said *zit*. Therefore I am not cool anymore. Q.E.D.

17   I possess exactly that type of blemish above my upper lip. It proves that I am juvenile, ergo a juvenile.

18   Fine, but you still owe us a demonstration of *exactly*.

19   It's futile to switch seats.

20   The world is the truth. That is true. So is my white t-shirt.

21   The truth has two aspects: fidelity and reality. They are the metaphysical duo.

22   We interrupt this philosophical program to pose a crucial question: What if you only had thirteen years, i.e., days to make your case, then *they* would judge you: could you keep your head and do it?

23   The world is all that is the head case.

24   Don't be so stupid. Only be a little stupid.

25   I am not a head case. I am Mia Stella, and I know it.

26   I am loyal to the truth. Otherwise, I am a traitor. I am Mia.

27   Cropped hair just long enough to be messy. A girl who is a wildman. A he-girl.

28   A man who is a wild girl. A manly girl. A wildchild. A girlyman. An ancient kid.

29   This might be too innocent.

30   This might be a throwback. Like Quisp cereal. They brought it back, it failed to thrive. The little Martian with the beanie with the individualistic propeller on it had to go back to Mars. He was autistic.

31   I went in search of a Mars bar.

32   I went in search of myself.

33   Mia Stella eats Mars bars. They have shiny black wrappers. Until they don't exist anymore.

34   Black ≠ yellow.

35   Are you innocent?

36   I don't know, should I be innocent?

37   My elbows keep hitting things which are cruel and hard to disprove.

38   Then are you experienced?

39   I don't know, should I be experienced?

40   The empirical cripple vs. the rational dolt. They could be capitalized and meet in a boxing match.

41   Transcendentally off-kilter wrists.

42   Corner dizziness, vertigo of the curb. A flashing imperative.

43   The irrational foot inside the boot or sneaker. It's the left one. You have to choose it.

44	Mia Stella committed a foot fault.

45	Bingo! Banishment by headbands and curfews.

46	It's good to have them hate you, it makes you young and energetic.

47	It is never too late to start again. So here.

48	The truth is all that is the instance. Alias substance.

49	Its two aspects are subjectivity and objectivity. Or fidelity and reality. But are these the same?

50	The truth is subjective, aka first person singular. Axiom of Subjectivity.

51	No subject without object. Axiom of Presentation.

52	Therefore the truth is also objective. Theorem of Objectivity. Alias Theorem of Normativity.

53	What about so-called private aka inner objects? Such as my thought that Quisp tasted better than Quake. Or my feeling of jumpiness?

54	They are true, you should admit them. They belong to the world.

55	Then what exactly are subject and object? And how could a feeling be an object?

56	By *objective* I do not mean absolute. Nor yet—God forbid!—intersubjective. I mean constitutive of the object. Some objects are private, but private has two meanings: only accessible to me or also accessible to you, even though you don't happen to perceive these objects, i.e., agree. Either way, the objects have reality.

57   The individual yields the norm all by itself. Via truth—its subjectivity. It isn't social or rational. It is first-personal.

58   But that doesn't answer our question, what exactly are—

59   By *God* we mean truth, it is the finite and temporal instance. Alias essence.

60   But that doesn't answer our question, what exactly—

61   By *we* we mean royalty. The philosopher-prince in exile.

62   But that doesn't answer our question, what—

63   By *we we* we mean you know what, ha!

64   Whoever knows, knows that he knows, and knows that he knows that he knows, and etc., said my papa. I replied, Huh? Piss off! He smiled calmly and gently.

65   Clearly and distinctly, my papa's name was Benedick. He was a bright light of reason.

66   But I was an inky dark shadow on him, and my stepmother banished me. Or because I had invalid inferences in my hair.

67   Schematically, my stepmother's name was Irma. She was a beacon of rationality.

68   I am a bastard, that is true. Officially, I am no son of anybody. Dub me Ismael.

69   Therefore my world is illegitimate. That does not mean it is false.

70   Issy, sissy, pissy.

71   *Sissy* means little sister or effeminate male, *pissy* means angry or irritable, *Issy* means—but why should I tell you? Ismael kept himself a secret.

72   Suddenly the paper clip leapt away, losing faith.

73   There exist paper clips.

74   Philosophers are afraid to be stupid. That keeps them from being smart. I am no philosopher.

75   If you tear your hair out, it will still be brown. Unless yellow.

76   The world contains two fundamental sides which are thought and thing. Or subjectivity and objectivity. A thing could be physical or not. It is the content of a thought.

77   The world is *my* world, because I am speaking. I, Ismael alias Mia, say *the world*. But is that a different I? Say, one outside? But how could there be such an I?

78   Furthermore, could this solo voice be a mistake? The universal voice is not the individual voice—although an individual can wield it.

79   Franz lost his voice. Then he piped up like Josephina. Also he was starving. He didn't sound as good as before.

80   Once Pavel Shvartz said Mia looked like a mouse, but he was psychedelically tripping.

81   That is a whole other kneepad.

82   The susceptible. *The Susceptible*. Ismael the susceptible. *Ismael the Susceptible*.

83   Fold it in like metaphysical origami.

84   Japanese sandwiches said hi.

85   Synthesis of the manifold is required for anything, but what if it's an illegal one?

86   Quit your fretting, state your point. A thud from the side.

87   That the world is the truth shows that it's dual-aspect. Doubly expressive.

88   Fidelity means the loyalty of sentences or thoughts. Reality means the thing to which they're loyal. Which could itself be yet another thought. For all true thoughts have both types of truth: fidelity and reality. Cf. my papa.

89   The world has two sides, neither side is metaphysically the favorite.

90   Once there was a man with two sons, the eldest destined to be a famous warrior, the youngest fated to be an obscure warrior. But he, the unglorified one, was the father's secret favorite.

91   White t-shirts are supposed to be the armor of purity. That is true.

92   But what if they have yellow armpits because they're old? White ≠ yellow.

93   The white t-shirt is true iff the white t-shirt.

94   Then scornfully *they* will laugh at me.

95   'The t-shirt is white' is true if and only if the t-shirt is white. That is called a *t-sentence*. Its standard form is, 'S' is true iff S—where S itself should be a sentence, according to them.

96   A t-shirt is not a sentence. Therefore a t-shirt is not a t-sentence. Such is valid reasoning.

97   However, truth is shaped like a T, it is the right angle, which has two directions. I.e., subjective and objective. Thus it is homomorphic with a t-shirt.

98   Conversely, the truth cannot be taken off like a t-shirt, it is always with you. Even if you are doubting, i.e., fearing. It's like the shirt and sleeves I saw tattooed on the handsome brunet street youth. The tattoo had the appearance of a mail shirt. Except made of fire. Dub him Sir Johnny, for Johnny the Human Torch, who cried, *Flame on!* and turned to flames when he was angry. He was Mia's favorite. Then there was his older sister Invisible Girl, she could turn invisible. But she couldn't get mad. Or stay it.

99   Jeanne d'Arc had cropped hair and wore true, i.e., bona fide armor. Probably she put on a helmet for battle. Still, she could hear God's voice through the metal. It was ringing. Also, through the flames that burned her up. They were theirs, not hers.

100   She was no traitor, she was loyal to God and the French, but I am a traitor, I am loyal to truth and the frank, otherwise I'm not. My hand is raised against everyone, even kin. Because I know that it is mine.

101   Then abruptly famished, I quit writing to eat. In the wilderness there exist hot dog stands. They could be Japanese.

*

102   Hunger equals claustrophobia plus gutsy centrifugal yearning.

103   Ismael lived in his size 6-petite hermit's cave, it was tonic, not Platonic or ironic. Yet breadless, sometimes airless. Those who lose their breath shall gain it.

104   Outside there might be nowhere to sit. Thus you roam.

105   Ismael was a wanderer heard by God.

106   Once there was a queen who had a favored son but thought it was a good idea, universally, to add on a little daughter. Since she couldn't properly conceive of one, she sent her husband the king to bed her maidservant. When the infant appeared, it supposedly gazed scornfully at the queen, who grew harsh with it. So the infant crawled away from home, its young true mama following alongside it. They hid in the wilderness and practiced resentment for some days. Then the truth spoke to the infant, saying, *Your father is your master, you should return to him.* So the child and mother returned and assumed their old position as unfavored interlopers. But such an assumption was provisional, since soon, the mama ran away, and later, the child was banished to the woods.

107   Should an infant fake a smile?

108   The king's and queen's names were Benedick Estella and Irma Kurt; their son's name was Ludovic Estelle, the maidservant's name was Selma Kirk Edgar, and the bastard girl's name was Mia Stella.

109   Then she became Ismael. I.e., the truth did.

110   Each element has a crucial metaphysical role to play in divine truth, the totality.

111   Individual things are elements of the world, which have different modes of presentation as features.

112   The modes of presentation are senses of the element, which is the referent.

113   There is no referent *behind* the senses, the referent is simply the set of its senses.

114   The senses are ways of *conceiving* the referent aka the element, but that is just what makes the element up. In the Godhead, which is the sum of all first person singular views.

115   When *he*, Benedick, said *mode*, he meant what I, Mia, mean by *element*. But also by *sense*, except he thought we know only two types: thought and extension.

116   Then I said *mode*, he said nothing. I stole his terms and I corrupted them. I might put myself on trial.

117   A sad or spastic mode. With the varnish chipped off. Feature presentation.

118   A desk or a table leg. I like wood. There's some in this place. Brown ≠ orange. Biconditional bald head.

119   Secretly, semantics and metaphysics are one and the same. Not rival brothers.

120   It's a secret because fools = fools. Why should I help them understand?

121   The identity of semantics and metaphysics harks back to the two aspects of truth (alias God alias substance).

122   Each mode of presentation has a subjective and an objective aspect: it presents the truth in two ways. Therefore each element—set of modes—does.

123   Knock-kneed maimed guy in bright blue and red Superman t-shirt. Words or things. In his early 30s. Still living with his mama and green beans. He's in my visual field. Verbal field. Veridical field. But also, he's external.

124   The one truth, the two aspects, the infinite elements with their infinite modes. Including the knock-kneed guy—say, Oscar Herbert.

125   Large vs. extra-large infinities. Like with eggs, it can be hard to tell the difference. Especially under pressure, with the judges all around.

126   Do the cardinality test, can they be set into a one-to-one correspondence? Like thoughts and things.

127   Don't go mathematical, you will become lost and deformed. Go elliptical or hyperbolic.

128   Rain with ankles qua hopeful raiment. Huh? Where are the flash cards?

129   By Georg, I think she's lost it!

130   Cantors are those who sing Hebrew songs and prayers. Whereas recanters are those who take sayings back. Such as wanderings. That is true, if not provable.

131   The synagogue judges expelled my papa, the Hebrews excommunicated him because he would not recant. They did it with a song, like in a Jewish opera.

132   Such as *The Magic Fruit Loop,* by Wolfgang Amschel Deus Moshe.

133   Then he, Benedick Estella, could flourish in his metaphysics. A mavericknik.

134   Metaphysically, everything was simpler for my father than it is for me. First, he posited one universal truth matching the one substance which exceeded and included it. Second, he minimized the I, his understanding of thought was strangely impersonal. Third, he held up rationality as the structure of the world. He was a true innocent.

135   I don't know, should I be my father?

136   Methodologically, everything was simpler for my father than it is for me. First, he followed geometry. Second, he wrote in Latin. Third, he believed in intellectual love of God or Nature, aka intuitive knowledge of Him.

137   The disorder of thoughts is the infection of things.

138   Such is *my* significant proposition.

139   One day I muttered my significant proposition to my papa but he didn't hear me. I was already alone in the woods. If he had heard me, he might have replied, *Mia, you are titillated and suffused.*

140   I mean defused.

141   Because I had cut off all my hair, and I possessed a left foot that pointed to the side instead of to the front.

142   No, that's not why.

143   His name was Benedick Estella, and he had two sons—one son Ludovic Estelle and one daughter Mia Stella—by different females. I already postulated that. Untame one, trim this! No! Ismael waved his hand to talk again, like in class.

144   Benedick Estella had shiny brown hair, his wife Irma Kurt had deep brown hair, their son Ludovic Estelle had umber brown hair, Benedick's maidservant Selma Kirk Edgar had glinting blonde hair, and their illegitimate child Mia Stella had dark blonde, i.e., dirty blonde hair. Therefore their philosophies.

145   Greasy metaphysics. Tousled semantics. Knotty ontology. Bird's nest aesthetics.

146   A bird, for example a canary. I don't know why. Yes you do. This yellow thing is really bugging me.

147   Desperation, yellow feathers; inspiration, yellow paper; perspiration, yellow armpits. I want something different now!

148   Aspiration's heavy breathing. Expiration's rapid breathing.

149   The shallow breaths of Franz. He was an old-world pseudo-crow. Therefore his dark hair.

150   This will never be perfected. I.e., real. I.e., true. But why must reality be perfect?

151   Fall heat wave, hot breeze, fetching girl in blue Keds and green flowery sun dress. X sings better than ZZ. Trees lighten up. Clauses saunter. A guy cursed because he had to, the derivation of things entailed it. *We should love what is necessary.* So said Herr Estella. *What if nothing is necessary,* said back Fräulein Stella.

152   In the Godhead of hair, all modes are true. That doesn't mean they are logical consequences.

153   Even if they are, it doesn't mean we should not hate them. Some hatred is good. For instance, hatred of some hatred. Some hatred is bad. For instance, hatred of some life.

154   Then the Persians decided to wipe out the Hebrews.

155   Then the Hebrews decided to white out the Persians.

156   We might perish in thirteen days, here in this Hebrew-plus-sized city. Wha-? It hit me like a bombshell. I am only named Stella, not the Persian variant.

157   Don't panic.

158   Don't be slavish.

159   Don't get tight.

160   A loosely strung bow makes a different sound.

161   Arrows flying everywhere.

162   *Raveling* also means unraveling.

163   As in philosophizing.

164   Ismael was lured back, then they laughed at him. Is that so terrible?

165   Ismael crept back to have somebody other than himself to fight. He raised his hand.

166   Mia likes to have enemies. They are steroids.

167   Resentment in the belly. Admiration in the shins. Aggression in the extremities.

168   If you did know that here is your hand, then would you be granted a rest? I do not think so.

169   Mia Stella is a great idea. But right now, I don't really feel like it.

170   Thirteen days is not an eternity. Neither is thirteen years. Thirteen seconds might be.

171   Metaphysics should convey desperation. Swear off analgesic philosophy!

172   The mailbox was stripped and left to die. It felt empty. A kid who learned to write his name ripped off my face. Sour milkiness in the café. Toddlers, shrieks, ethics. Bushy hair which could be symbolized in first-disorder logic. Days are for diving. Outside, I try to be a sidewalk crack. People would avoid me for good luck. Precocity in the girl, immaturity in the adult. In the distance, a great sullen castle which is a sanatorium for mind-body invalids. Fear and desire. Its proper name is Igor aka Ingvar Burton. The Axiom of Misery entails doom at 5:00 AM. The world has things which argue back. Bite the abstractions. *Ideas with teeth marks are unacceptable,* ruled a schoolteacher. The abstractions practiced gulping down everything. But I suffer from a swallowing phobia. So I chew everything very strenuously. Like Franz Koughka did, before he went to live in Igor. They put him on a strict Yoo-hoo diet. I am a thing.

173   Then rainfall hit the dusk, slapped the sidewalk around. Bruises bloomed under my eyeballs.

174   It's raining, and I don't believe it's raining. Huh? Geordie Muir's paradox. The limit of the first person. Truth qua belief.

175   Or I could rip the *Book of Esther* out of the Bible, shove her into my notebook, carry her with me and think about the destruction of the aliens, which is also hard to swallow.

176   *Booklet of Ismael.*

177   *Pamphlet of Mia.*

178   *Tractate of Stella.*

179   Maybe everything is necessary, but the *Ethics* never had its head shaved or was forced to breathe bad air. Still it knew things.

180   Hebrews qua birds. Yellow canaries. Yellow stars. Yellow Stella.

181   I think now you might be being stupid, with fear and fumbling.

182   Then all the first person singulars were collected into one set—the annulled set. Ismael saw how transience was the key to truth. The truth is mortal. But that should be a different volume. A heavy one, vs. this leaflet, which is meant to be lightweight. With loose pages.

*

183   Snow or opaque white marbles with ribbony orange streaks. Or spaldeens or keyholes. Or that thought about the versions.

184   Just be honest.

185   Altered impulse collar. Wires of hair.

186   Nervous. Nervy.

187   The truth's two aspects: fidelity and reality. Subjectivity and objectivity must be different.

188   Draw a graph with the horizontal I-axis (for the I) and the vertical W-axis (for the world), so the truth is two-dimensional. Subject on left, object on right, reality above, fidelity below.

189   The world is bigger than reality. Because the truth is.

190   Subjective facts and thoughts don't equal objective facts and thoughts. But they're still *objects* for some subject—by Axiom of Presentation. Thus some objects are themselves subjective, not objective.

191   That is weird.

192   Subject vs. subjective vs. subjectivity!

193   Street shouts and chirps. Interference. Contra inference strings. Like my grey sweater vest. Maybe it could help. It has no sleeves attached.

194   Then there's belief: isn't *it* the true fidelity? The other two require it.

195   So the truth has *three* aspects: fidelity, veracity and reality.

196   What Mia called *fidelity* before, she should have called *veracity*. In the graph, it's below.

197   As for the new fidelity—the faith of the I—is it a third axis or simply the origin (0,0)?

198   But shouldn't the origin be the I itself? So the I-axis was really the F-axis (for faith)?

199   I don't know how to draw my picture yet!

200   Then *they* snickered. I stuck my tongue out like a neck. Balled my hands into fists. Got closer—

201   Forget them! Wrestling's solitary.

202   If agon, then agonize. If agonize, then anguish. Ergo, if agon, then anguish. The private anguish argument.

203   The private anguish *argh*!

204   Tight place like a strangled throat.

205   Cf. anxious.

206   That bird was trying to get out of my chest again.

207   Whereof one can't be silent, thereof one must speak.

208   I said that to my elder brother, but he misheard me.

209   He was 15 and I was 13. I was circumcised, then I ran away. Unless I ran away just beforehand.

210   Once a smart girl named Mia was banished to the wilderness of her room by her cold obscure stepmother Irma or perhaps by the two family servants, Boris and Georgy.

211   This was because 1) she had been playing with her elder brother Ludovic, teaching him songs about subjectivity, 2) her papa favored her, despite her deviant ideas, and might give her all of his wealth.

212   She was sent to her room with no milk and cookies, *a fortiori* no Sauerbraten supper. Father, stepmother and half brother faintly audible on the other side; her mama, the housemaid, had run off long ago, shirking her responsibilities for the sake of some fantastic religion. Meanwhile Boris and Georgy brought rules and water once a day, to keep Mia alive but stupefied, mechanical, hollow.

213   Pages passed like years. Mia starved slowly yet decisively. She wasted away until she was thin as piece of paper and dead like one with bad writing done in good handwriting. It was then that Mia summoned up wild force and hurled herself out of the window. She soared off on a Corona Zephyr (olive brown with Mars black keys), finally came to alight on a tree branch in a wood—a wannabe leaf. Flapped to the ground, but at least now she was free.

214   Then God came as the truth and said, *See, I heard you. I hear everything.*

215   And Mia understood. She said, *I am Ismael.*

216   Mia wrote *Ismael* because she rebelled even against proper spelling. Made up alternatives.

217   Ludovic was a terrible speller, and he felt ashamed of it. Mia was terrible at handwriting, but she felt proud. She refused to take penmanship class.

218   Ditto for typing.

219   Ludovic was the noble yet plainly dressed son, Mia remained ignoble and childishly attired. In a V-neck. Yet she developed.

220   13 is important. Today I am a Mia—alias an Ismael!

The Felix

I.   *If God*

<u>Definitions</u>

1D   Because of itself vs. depending on the haircut.

2D   We had a thought which was a girdle for a word.

3D   Truth qua substance?

4D   The attributes are Rockettes.

5D   The modes are the Rockettes' metaphysical hair follicles, all over their bodies.

6D   By *God* is meant truth, it is the infinite yet temporal imperfection.

7D   Redhead, brunette, blonde. Benedict de Spinoza was a brunet with a Jewfro. It grew into heavy metal.
   Exp.: Men can be brunets but they are shorter.

8D   That thing is called *free* which has a willful disorder.
   Exp.: By *eternity* I don't understand anything.

<u>Axioms</u>

1A   I am Greta or I am God.

2A   We are able to conceive of ourselves as Myra.

3A   That could have no effect, therefore be a lost cause.

4A   The concepts of Greta, Myra and God intersected, although their spelling didn't.

5A   A truth makes an irritation like a possibility and hurts.

6A   My name is Greta Felix, but I do not have to exist. Instead, I could make up a reductio. If I want to.

Propositions

1P   Dusk dripped onto the fire escape, the mad delivery man below iterated mechanically *Liar . . . liar . . .*
   Demo.: Nerve strings of the eyes and ears.

2P   To be akin is to share an attribute such as the brunette Rockette or the musical key of B-minor.

3P   *Greta* is an old-fashioned name and could name a Rockette from the childhood of Greta: she would be different.
   Cor.: Similarly *Myra*.

4P   On the stage of life it can be difficult to perform.
   Demo.: The dent in my book matches the dent in my forehead. By 5A, we are very irritable. Books have spines which can be cracked. Piano keys can be cracked. I could be a keyboard. The ivories turned into yellows. Greta's fast hair. I do not know if I will be the same length as Spinoza lying down. He grew sickly from a lung infection. He was already short. I am short. Hungry. Must quit thinking and eat. I will use my hands with the long musical fingers. Indivisibility of extended substance, no removal of extremities. I know that here is my hand, because I plink with it. So said Greta before the terrible accident. I plink, therefore I am. Her hands got slammed in the pianoforte metaphysics. The order of thoughts is the order of dings. Greta is mutilated and refused. Is *refused* passive or active?

5P It is time for our cripples' supper now.

6P Nobody is a whole.
   Demo: By 5P, we are all crippled.

*

7P Today is another day, I am Greta and I am insubstantial.

8P *Greta* is a name whose meaning is fixed, but Greta's meaning isn't. Therefore names are stunt doubles, sometimes they perish. Or necessary lies.
  Schol. 1: Infinity is a chaos which causes a semantic and metaphysical headache or a rapture. *Myra* means abundance.
  Demo.: Until I knew that I was secretly Myra, riotous thoughts pounded my head, giving me a terrible pain of resistance. Pain is one form of proof. With the pathological consequence. But every instance is infinite. Having infinite possible reality, thus an infection or invention.
  Schol. 2: In truth everything is insubstantial. Perhaps unsubstantiated. It could feel good not to carry any weight, as in a fairy tale. Street sweeping vehicle spins dirt and trash *da capo*. A proposition will save you or it will release you. The condition of possibility of truth is a piano hammer which hits a nerve string such as B♯ or F. The string vibrates. Emission of tone. Brief.